Bird in the Nest

Bird in the Nest

Bill Oddie

and

Peter Holden

Recommended by the RSPB

By arrangement with BBC Enterprises Ltd

ROBSON BOOKS

First published in Great Britain in 1995 by Robson Books Ltd,
Bolsover House, 5–6 Clipstone Street, London W1P 8LE

British Library Cataloguing in Publication Data
A catalogue record for this title is available from the British Library

Designed by Linda Wade

ISBN 0 86051 983 X

Set in Palatino by Columns Design and Production Services Ltd, Reading
Printed in Great Britain by Butler & Tanner Ltd,
London and Frome

For Hilary and the rest of the *Bird in the Nest* team

ACKNOWLEDGEMENTS

Our thanks to all the *Bird in the Nest* team: Hilary Jeffkins, Roy Chapman, Sara Ford, James Honeyborne, Lloyd Buck, Ruth Flowers, Fran Phipps, Pamela Jackson, Sarah Byatt, Rita Aspinall, Charlie Hamilton James, Peter Bassett, Steven Greenwood, Susan Flood, Melissa Blandford, Alison Young, Geoffrey Stafford, Andrew McClenaghan, John Norman, Geoff Vian, Ian Stacey, Paul Cheary, Ian Powell, Andrew Anderson, Mark Yates, Rod Lewis, Tony Briskham, David Liquorice, Nigel Abbott, Alan Hoida, Peter Belcher, Martyn Harries, Peter Davies, Paul Bond and Steven Faux.

Thanks also to The Hawk and Owl Trust and all the nest site owners.

CONTENTS

INTRODUCTION

I'm writing this just after finishing the second series of *Bird in the Nest*: and what a pleasure it was to work on it. I can definitely say that this was the most enjoyable 'birdy' job I've ever done. But it *was* a job . . . work in fact, and hard work at that. No doubt Peter Holden and myself had a slightly less stressful time than the technical crew but the fact remains that, at the end of a week's live television, we were left feeling, well, pretty exhausted. Tired, but happy, as they say. There wasn't a lot of time off between broadcasts but, when we did get a few minutes' break, we tended to stay in 'The Birdmobile' and gaze at the pictures on our little monitor screens, switching from nest to nest. It wasn't that we were too weary to go for a walk – we really couldn't tear ourselves away. We remained equally enthralled by the birds and intrigued and impressed by the incredibly elaborate set-up of cameras, cables, transmitters and expertise that is the trademark of the BBC Natural History Unit. For my own part, I couldn't help feeling terribly lucky to have got this far. A lifelong hobby had become an immensely satisfying job. I also found myself thinking back to my childhood and how my involvement – no, obsession – with birds and bird-watching had first begun. The truth is, that the pictures seemed rather appropriate. They brought back a lot of memories.

You see, it all began – as indeed do birds themselves – with an egg. I was living in Rochdale, near Manchester, aged six, when I had my first close encounter. Literally. A chum gave me a Canary's egg.

I wrapped it in cotton wool, put it in a matchbox, put the matchbox in my back pocket, climbed over a wall, sat on the top, and ended up with yolk-stained shorts. It was hardly a traumatic incident, but I've never forgotten it. From that day on, I felt a close affinity with birds, and in particular with eggs . . .

The next significant formative experience occurred under the privet hedge that grew in front of our terraced house in Sparthbottom's Road. What a great Lancastrian name eh? What's more, back in them days – the late 1940s – the streets were cobbled, the women wore shawls, the men flat hats, and the kids carried Hovises to the accompaniment of brass bands. And I used to play football with a bundle of rags. Then, one day, a wayward volley ended up under the hedge. As I crawled into the bushes to retrieve the 'ball', I became aware that I was being watched by a pair of beady little eyes. There, above my head, was a nest. As I stretched up to inspect it, a bird flew off. I peered inside, and saw four exquisite sky-blue eggs. I thought they were brilliant. Better than a squashed Canary's any day. I wanted to know what bird had laid them and so I asked my dad to buy me a bird book. To his eternal credit, he did. In those days, there was only one: *The Observer's Book of Birds*. I rummaged through it, hoping to recognize my bird. All I knew was that it looked like a sparrow and it lived in a hedge. On page 132 I found it: 'Hedge Sparrow'. Good name. I had made my first successful identification and I was hooked. The next step was to save up my pocket money to buy a second book. Alas, this time it was a rather more sinister volume: *The Observer's Book of Birds' Eggs*. I returned to the Hedge Sparrow's nest and took one of the sky-blue jewels. Thus began my egg collection and my life of crime.

To be honest, it would have been a pretty weird schoolboy who didn't go birds' nesting back in the late 1940s. It was one of those things that affirmed your masculinity. Like scrumping apples, firing catapaults, or pulling girls' pigtails. To be fair, we had a pretty rigorous code of conduct. We only took one egg, preferably from an incomplete clutch (so that the embryo hadn't started to develop) and we despised and indeed gave a damn good hiding to any boy found 'ragging', or wilfully destroying, nests. Nevertheless, egg collecting was a destructive activity, which nowadays is thankfully illegal, and almost unheard of amongst youngsters, though it is, sadly, still practised by grown men, whose collecting instincts have taken a particularly warped and insidious turn. Meanwhile, however, back when I was a lad, I knew that egg collecting was wrong but I was so obsessed that I really needed a severe dose of aversion therapy to teach me the wickedness of my ways. I got it.

One evening, I was lurking around in the 'rough', alongside the local golf course, when I almost stepped into a nest containing no less than fourteen large, golden-brown eggs. The grass was soggy and the eggs were cold, damp and clearly abandoned. I immediately deduced that they had been laid by what was now an ex-Pheasant. Presumably the poor bird had been felled by a fatal shot from either a twelve bore or a number nine iron. Anyway, it was clear that these eggs were not about to hatch into baby Pheasants, and I therefore felt no guilt at breaking my 'single-egg' rule, I took two.

An hour later, I was back in my kitchen admiring my trophies and still wondering how long they'd been lying unattended. I was about to find out. Now, fellow erstwhile juvenile-delinquent egg collectors will no doubt feel a twinge of remorseful recognition when I remind them of what you had to do with your eggs before adding them to your collection. You had to blow them. Right? This entailed poking a small hole in one end with a sharp pin (or a miniature awl, if you were a real professional) and a slightly larger hole in the other end. You then applied your lips to the small hole, and blew hard. With any luck – and a little effort – the yolk and white of the egg would then shoot out of the large hole, leaving the shell hollow and remarkably strong. However, in this case, with no luck – and despite a great deal of effort – nothing whatsoever came out. Except a rather foul smell. Clearly these eggs had been there a very long time indeed. Nevertheless, I continued to blow and blow. My eyes bulged, my cheeks inflated like bellows, and my face turned a ripe shade of purple but it was clear that the inside of the egg was fetid, gooey and utterly unblowable.

What *could* I do? Well, back in those days, I was not

RSPB/Mark Hamblin

A Hedge Sparrow or Dunnock.

only a delinquent, I was also extremely stupid. Obviously, I was never going to be able to *blow* the stuff out. So . . . there was obviously only one alternative. I would have to . . . Yep, you've got it. I held my nose in one hand, and the egg in the other, and *sucked* the evil contents into my mouth. I then spat into the sink, and placed the egg into its cotton wool compartment. Then I repeated the process with the second egg. Next, I stuck on little labels. And, finally, I stood back to admire my newly enhanced collection . . . and threw up over the lot!

It was at that moment that I finally gave up egg collecting. Even now, the taste still lingers, and believe me, I have never been able to look a Pheasant in the face again. Let alone the other end. But there

was a positive outcome: from that day on I vowed to become a bird-watcher.

Obviously egg collecting *is* wrong, but at least the long hours watching breeding birds and tracking them to their cunningly concealed nests had taught me one valuable discipline: patience. It was an attribute that was to come in extremely useful when, in my late teens, my bird-watching took on a rather more scientific purpose and I became qualified as a ringer, that is, to catch and ring birds with small metal bands so their movements and migrations can be studied. Ringing takes considerable skill. Nobody is allowed to do it without proper training and a certificate of competence. It takes even more precise knowledge and care to find and ring young birds in the nest. Discovering the nests in the first place is often difficult enough but then the youngsters have to be ringed at exactly the correct time. If the nestlings are too small, the ring will fall off. Too large and the birds may spill out of the safety of the nest before their time. It was a tricky business but, nevertheless, I found that, having acquired this skill, the rewards were immense. Not because I felt that I was contributing that much to the cause of ornithological research, but because of the sheer sense of joy and wonder at getting to know birds at such close quarters. I loved them.

I shall never forget when I held my first Ringed Plover because the bird was so serene and gentle. Nor shall I forget my first Puffin, because it was a vicious little blighter. As I attempted to clip on its nice shiny ring, it lacerated my wrists with its needle-sharp claws. I looked like I'd been attacked by a werewolf, but the bird had – so to speak – made its point. And a very sharp point it was too. But the experiences all taught me to respect and admire the birds – for the ingenuity of their nest building, the amazing devotion and tenacity of the adults in defending and bringing up their families and the sheer charm of the youngsters. Some were undeniably ugly: only its parents could consider a young Pigeon or Shag to be a pretty baby. Whilst others were undeniably cute. But all were fascinating. They were quite simply wonderful to look at.

Frankly, it sometimes bothers me that many bird-watchers today are so obsessed with rarity chasing – or twitching – and with the scientific analysis of ornithology that they perhaps tend to be unmoved by the sheer visual appeal of birds, and especially young birds. It's almost as if finding them endearing is considered a bit 'soppy'. Fortunately, the public ('does he mean us?' to quote Derek Jameson) tends to be less self conscious. There's nothing to be embarrassed about in letting out the odd 'aaaw'. Or indeed the occasional 'yuk'. Almost child-like reactions perhaps, but entirely natural, like the birds themselves.

Bird in the Nest has been called an 'avian soap opera'. Well, I don't know if it's a tribute to the appeal of birds or of soap operas (or both?) but certainly the viewing figures compared pretty favourably with the human versions. Personally, I find the inhabitants of a Blue Tits' nest box far more endearing than the regulars at the Queen Vic and I'd certainly prefer to have Great Spotted Woodpeckers as my Neighbours but, in any case, it seems they certainly make equally popular telly.

Anyway, I really should stop rambling and reminiscing and get on with the writing (Peter has just phoned to say he's finished two chapters already). So . . . just as doing the series brought back memories for me, I hope this book brings back memories for you.

Thanks for watching and now thanks for reading too.

Warning! Don't Try This At Home

Just as bird ringing requires training and a licence, so does some bird photography and filming or, usually, video taping these days. In this book, we will tell you how the BBC got their cameras into the nests, as it were. It will be obvious that the techniques require a great deal of care and expertise. They also require legal permission. So *please* don't be tempted to have a go yourself.

This doesn't mean, of course, that you can't encourage birds to nest in your garden, or indeed study and photograph them. It's obvious from the stacks of letters and pictures that we've received that it's happening all over the country. Good. All we're saying is, do take great care not to disturb the birds when they are nesting. The consequences really can be tragic. An adult bird flushed off her eggs may leave them so that they get chilled and they won't hatch, or she may desert the nest altogether. Or the eggs may be left unattended just long enough for them to be taken by lurking predators such as squirrels, rats, crows, jays or magpies (fortunately though, at least, there aren't so many naughty schoolboys like the young Bill Oddie around these days). Keeping the parents away from nestlings can be just as disastrous. It deprives the young of food and warmth and the result can be fatal.

It's a pretty good rule to say: 'look, but don't touch'. Though of course there might be emergencies, when a little human intervention can save the day (and the birds). More advice on that on pages 120–21.

Otherwise, the more involved people get with their birds the better. Apart from the pleasure it gives to us, and the protection it gives to the birds, it can also

contribute all sorts of valuable information. There are plenty of opportunities to get involved in garden bird surveys. It adds to our knowledge and it is vital to conservation. And by all means get those cameras out, but do be aware that close-up nest photography of certain species is illegal without a licence.

So, what we're saying is: watch, snap, sketch, study, feed, care and enjoy . . . but, please leave the tricky stuff to the Beeb. Ta.

So, Whose Idea Was It Then?

Like so many successful ideas for TV series, *Bird in the Nest* sort of evolved. In fact, amazing pictures from places where cameras shouldn't theoretically be able to go have been a feature of natural history programmes for a surprisingly long time. Older readers and viewers whose memories go back to the days of Armand and Michaela Denis and Hans and Lotte Hasse (both of whom, incidentally, we remember well enough to do passable impersonations of, though we're not saying who gets to wear the blond wigs!) may also recall the true sense of astonishment when Heinz Sielmann first showed us what went on inside Woodpeckers' nests. When *was* that? Well, not that long after the Second World War, probably still in black and white, in fact. Certainly, in those days, the cameras were pretty big and cumbersome, and the set ups correspondingly awkward. It was pioneering stuff but, since then, things have progressed at an astonishing rate.

Nowadays, some cameras are so tiny that they can get inside the Woodpeckers themselves. Frankly, miraculous images have become so commonplace that we tend to take them for granted. Let's face it, once you've seen a living embryo moving inside an egg, or a miniature David Bellamy clambering around in a daffodil, or David Attenborough lying in a termites' mound, it's unlikely that baby birds in a nest – even if they are inside a nest box – will strike you as particularly amazing from a technical point of view. As it happens, such pictures are still a pretty impressive achievement but, nevertheless, it was surely not the 'how on earth do they do that?' element that made *Bird in the Nest* something a bit

magical. So what *was* the special ingredient? It was *live*.

The real seeds of the concept were probably sown back in the late 1980s, during another series made by the BBC Natural History Unit called *Wild Britain*. Several key people worked on that show. Among the producers were Alistair Fothergill and Mike Beynon and the researchers included Hilary Jeffkins. The programme was studio based which, in TV speak, means that the presenters sit in the studio, usually behind desks, and introduce filmed (or videotaped) items featuring the wildlife, often involving roving reporters who seem to be having all the fun. One element of *Wild Britain* that seemed to be the most fun of all was a series of live bulletins from various birds' nests, showing exactly what was going on, as it actually happened. Hilary recalls that these were the bits that the viewers seemed to particularly enjoy. To such an extent that the studio-based part of the programmes became shorter and shorter and no doubt the studio-based presenters became more and more envious of the outside reporters. As it happens, one of us was a live-nest commentator on the programme in the shape of a young (well, younger) man from The Royal Society for the Protection of Birds called Peter Holden.

The passing of those years brings us to 1993. Alistair Fothergill had now risen to the splendid height of Head of the Natural History Unit. Hilary Jeffkins was a producer and Mike Beynon was still having brilliant ideas. In fact, he was still having the same brilliant idea that had been so successful in *Wild Britain*. Hilary again recalls that it was Mike

BBC/José Schell

Peter, Bill and the Birdmobile

who was convinced that a series of live broadcasts from birds' nests spread over a whole week, would make fascinating viewing. He suggested the idea to Alistair who, since he was now the boss, was in a position to give it the official seal of approval. Hilary certainly needed no persuading to accept the invitation to produce the series.

It only remained to convince the ultimate power at the BBC – the Controller – that the programme would attract sufficient numbers of viewers to justify the considerable airtime and the not inconsiderable expense. Other live watches had proved pretty popu-

lar, indeed, so much so that the concepts had been getting bigger and bigger. The rather cosily domestic, and relatively modest, *Fox Watch* and *Badger Watch* had escalated through ever more ambitious projects, culminating in the spectacular notion of *Africa Watch* (and you don't get much bigger than Africa!). Mind you, as it happened, the big game was often less inclined to perform for the cameras than their less prima donna-ish British cousins. Viewers of *Africa Watch* may recall a number of bulletins involving slightly weary and sweaty reporters, perched on their Land Rovers, sheltering in the shade of an Acacia tree, telling us that we should have been here earlier. It was then that we realized that not only does 'the lion sleep tonight', but most of the day as well. But that's live telly for you. You never know what's going to happen. Possibly nothing at all . . .

Anyway, it may well be that broadcasts on the scale of *Africa Watch* represented something of an unsurpassable peak. Where do you go next? *World Watch*? *Moon Watch*? *Universe Watch*? No doubt the Natural History Unit would boldly go wherever it was sent and make a brilliant job of it. But would the British viewing public feel quite so involved? And wouldn't it get awfully expensive? It may well be that some of these thoughts were in the Controller's mind at the time, for it seems that, in 1993, he was feeling disposed towards a greater emphasis on British wildlife. So whether it was patriotism, the promise of popular appeal, or the fact that it was relatively cheap – whatever the reasons – *Bird in the Nest* was duly commissioned.

It would certainly be the direct opposite of the huge productions. Instead of the wide open spaces of the African plains and the impressive, yet perhaps rather impersonal, spectacles of huge herds of animals, *Bird in the Nest* would focus very specifically and intimately on its subjects. The viewer would really get to know them as individuals, characters, if you like. It was at this point, probably, that this phrase 'avian soap opera' was coined. It was particularly apt since – unlike most of the previous live watches, which had been one-day affairs – *Bird in the Nest* would be spread over a whole week. A soap opera indeed. With daily episodes. But no script. And live.

By early in 1994, it remained only for Hilary and Alistair to decide on the casting. The humans were probably relatively easy. Between the two of us, Peter Holden had clearly passed his unwitting audition on *Wild Britain* and was unanimously appointed as the 'expert'. We have never heard any more elaborate explanation of Bill Oddie's appointment than that he was chosen to provide a 'contrast' to Peter. Whether this was a compliment or an insult, only the BBC can tell us. And they ain't saying nuthin'!

Then came the rather more difficult part of the casting: the birds. It was decided that the series would feature five nests. But which five? There were rather a lot to choose from . . .

Blue Tit nest box.

So Many Nests – Those That Didn't Appear on TV

If asked to describe a bird's nest most people would probably imagine a cup-shaped object made of grass and wedged in a bush or tree. And they would be right, because there are lots of nests that look just like that, but there are many more which don't.

With about 9,000 species of birds in the world there is an amazing variety of nests. So far *Bird in the Nest* has looked at only 12. The nests chosen have been sites which allow the BBC Natural History Unit to put in their latest cameras, lights and microphones, but there are lots of other types of nest, some of which would present an even greater challenge to the Unit.

This chapter is all about the sorts of nest we have *not* included in the programmes and illustrates the different strategies that birds have evolved for protecting their eggs and rearing their young.

THE NO-NEST NEST

Some birds don't bother with a nest. Emperor Penguins, for example, hold their egg on top of their webbed feet until it hatches. This has the advantage that the bird can move around, albeit slowly, and take the egg along too. As Emperors incubate during the Antarctic winter we were quite glad this species was not chosen for the series.

Another group of birds that does not bother with making a nest has the sinister-sounding scientific name of 'brood-parasites'. In Britain we have just one, the Cuckoo, which simply lays its eggs into nests of other birds but there are a few other brood-parasites elsewhere in the world.

The Guillemot doesn't really have a nest either. It nests on small ledges of sheer sea cliffs and its egg is laid on to the bare rock. The egg is very pointed and

Guillemot: no nest, just a ledge.

if knocked it is likely to spin rather than roll into the sea.

The Ringed Plover is a small wading bird which, like many other waders, doesn't build a 'proper' nest. It lays its eggs in a scrape (a small hollow scraped in the pebbles on a beach) and then sits tight. If an adult has to leave the nest, it relies on the fact that the beautifully camouflaged eggs are likely to be overlooked by a predator. Young Ringed Plovers are covered with down when they hatch and they are able to run about, so the scrape is quickly abandoned.

Nightjar: perfect camouflage is essential for ground nesters.

A very different ground-nesting bird is the Nightjar, a nocturnal summer visitor from Africa which relies on its camouflaged plumage to remain unseen during the day. Again no nest is built and the eggs are laid into a depression in the ground. In this case the young stay in the same place after they have hatched and remain there for more than two weeks.

Perhaps the most remarkable no-nest nest is that of the Fairy Tern, a snowy white seabird of tropical oceans. It lays its single egg in a small depression in a tree branch. When the young tern hatches it stays in position until old enough to fly.

KEEPING IT SIMPLE

If a bird is going to build a nest off the ground then the most simple structure can be created by taking a few twigs, lodging them in a bush and then laying the eggs on top. Some birds do just that. A Woodpigeon's nest is a very flimsy affair and if you look from underneath you can often see the sky through the nest. Pigeons are not the best house-keepers either and, as time passes, the birds' droppings start to build up and help to hold the nest together.

In a different league altogether is the Osprey. It, too, builds a simple nest of sticks at the top of a tall tree but it uses large sticks and its nest may be used for many years. Also the Osprey goes on adding to the nest each year, so an old nest may eventually measure a metre and a half across and be one or two metres tall.

Fairy Tern: making a very careful landing!

SO MANY VARIATIONS ON A THEME

Simple cup-shaped nests come in many different forms and are often very intricate.

The smallest nest of all is a cup-shaped nest made by a Hummingbird: it is just 2 cm across. Among the largest are those built by Crows, made from sticks of various sizes and lined with plant material and wool. If you look up at a Rook's nest on a windy March day, you will realize just how well they have been built because at that time of year they will either contain eggs or small young. Now there's a challenge for the BBC . . .

Hummingbird: the tiniest nest and eggs.

In Britain, the smallest nest is built by the Goldcrest. The nest is round and cup-shaped and very delicate: it has an outer layer of cobwebs, moss and lichens, a middle layer, also of moss and lichen, and an inner lining of feathers and hair. The whole nest is about 9 cm across and the inner cup only 5 cm wide.

Blackbirds build cup-shaped nests of straw and grasses and incorporate mud into the design. The nest is then lined with fine grasses. The Song Thrush also uses twigs, grasses and moss for the main structure and then a lining made from mud, dung and rotten wood.

PUTTING A ROOF ON

Cup-shaped nests may be popular with many species but some go one better and put a roof on. The roof is not a separate structure, it is part of the design, improves protection and, in some cases, increases camouflage.

The Long-tailed Tit builds a beautifully camouflaged, domed nest (the shape of a small rugby ball) of moss, lichen and spiders' webs. The nest, which has an entrance hole in the side, is lined with up to 2,000 feathers and is suspended in a bush. The material is flexible and strong enough to hold up to twelve young tits but with no room for a camera.

Long-tailed Tit: the nest is an exquisite ball of lichens, spiders' webs and feathers.

A very different domed nest is built by the Magpie. It is a large nest built in a tall bush or tree and made of loosely woven twigs with a hole or two in the side. Inside, an inner nest is built of grasses, mud, roots and hair. Often the chosen tree is one that has thorns and the whole nest appears to have been designed to keep BBC cameras out.

LIFE IN A HOLE

Bird in the Nest has looked at several birds which nest in holes of one kind or another. But there are many other birds which nest in holes.

Puffins nest in burrows on sea cliffs. They may take over a rabbit burrow or they may dig their own. But Puffins are not the only seabird nesting underground on the cliffs of western Britain. The Manx Shearwater winters off the coast of South America and returns to British and Irish waters to breed. It spends the daylight hours out at sea and only comes ashore after dark and, like the Puffin, lays its egg in a burrow underground.

Bill Oddie

Puffin: they nest underground, often in old rabbit burrows.

Our Woodpeckers make impressive nests, but the Hornbills of Africa and Asia go even further. They select a natural hole in a tree or cliff and then start to make the entrance smaller with mud and their own droppings. Once the hole is the right size the female enters and walls herself inside leaving only a small slit for food to be brought. There she will stay to incubate the eggs while the food is delivered by the male. In some species the female remains inside until the young are ready to fly. Other females break out earlier, but the young then wall themselves up with their own droppings. Now that would make a good *Bird in the Nest*!

RSPB/Colin Carver

Woodpecker: they excavate their nest hole.

We don't have Hornbills in Britain, but we do have Nuthatches and they have some of the same habits. They choose a hole, often an old Woodpecker's hole, and the female makes it smaller with wet mud or clay being hammered into place until it sets almost like concrete. This prevents larger species from taking over the hole or attacking the young.

Nuthatches also like using nest boxes, but they do have a problem because the hole is usually the right size. The instinct to plaster with mud is so strong that the female plasters round, but not over, the hole and round some of the joints in the wood. Some Nuthatches even plaster the roof inside and out.

EDIBLE NESTS

Perhaps one of the strangest materials for a nest is saliva, which is used by several species of Swift. The Palm Swift of Africa sticks its nest to the undersides of leaves using saliva.

Swifts are not able to land and take off easily from the ground and therefore their nest material needs to be gathered in flight. The saliva is used to stick it together.

The nests of some species of Swiftlets in Asia are made up almost entirely of a special saliva produced by the birds for the purpose of nest building. It is this substance which is valued by the Chinese as a delicacy to form the basis of 'bird's nest soup'.

LIVING TOGETHER

While a great many birds set up a personal territory in which to feed and rear their young, others choose to live together in colonies.

Even in some colonies there are territories. A Gannet colony may look like a tight squash, but the nests are carefully spaced so that birds are out of pecking distance from each other. Some Tern colonies start with the nests being spaced out across a beach, but when the young become mobile they join together in large, moving crêches. How the parents know which young one to feed is one of those mysteries, but it probably has something to do with recognizing individual voices.

It is not unusual for small birds to build their nests in the nest of a larger species. Tree and House Sparrows, for example, will nest among the sticks at the base of a Rook's or Heron's nest. But perhaps the best example is that of the Hamerkop.

A Gannet colony: how do they find their own nest amongst this lot?

BBC/Brian Lightfoot

The Hamerkop is a relatively small stork-like bird of southern Africa which builds a massive nest in the fork of a tree. It may take months to build and inside the metre-wide nest is a chamber and an entrance tunnel, both plastered with mud. The final structure is so strong that it is said it can take the weight of a heavy man standing on top.

The Hamerkop's nest is in demand, the outer structure is home to many small birds and other larger species will take over if they have a chance. Verreaux's Eagle Owl, Barn Owl and Grey Kestrel will use abandoned nests as will Egyptian Goose, Monitor Lizards, Spitting Cobra and Genets.

FLOATING OUT OF DANGER

In J M Barrie's *Peter Pan* there is a reference to the never-never bird with its floating nest, which someone has identified as a Great-crested Grebe. We're not sure how reliable this identification is, but certainly these grebes do build a floating nest which has some very real advantages.

The Great-crested Grebe's nest is made from water weed and other plants growing in the water and is usually anchored to plants or branches.

Grebes are beautifully evolved for swimming and diving, their legs being set far back on their body, but this makes it hard for them to move on land, therefore a floating nest is ideal. It is also protection from predators as most dangers are likely to come from the land. Perhaps most important, a floating nest is also protection from rising, and falling, water levels.

MAKING IT WITH MUD

Bird in the Nest included the Swallow and its mud nest in the first series, but other birds use mud and some of them build much more elaborate structures than the Swallow's shallow saucer.

The House Martin is a familiar summer visitor to towns and villages, as it has almost abandoned nesting on cliffs in favour of nesting under the eaves of houses. The nest is made of tiny mud pellets and, provided it doesn't fall down, it will be used year after year. Young House Martins spend most of their lives looking out of the entrance hole, so if BBC cameras went in to show us the inside story we would only see the tail end!

Bill Oddie

Great-crested Grebe: the floating nest copes with fluctuating water levels, but they can still flood after very heavy rain.

A much more dramatic mud nest is made by the Ovenbird of South America which builds a huge, thick-walled structure with an entrance tunnel and nesting chamber. Now it would be fascinating to know what went on inside *that* edifice.

MASTER BUILDERS

The Weavers are a group of birds which includes the familiar House Sparrow. As their name suggests, most build elaborate nests, although the House Sparrow seems to be rather a failure.

Some weavers weave a separate nest chamber and also a tunnel up to a metre long for the birds to get in and out, and sometimes a ridge is woven to stop the eggs rolling out. Several species include mud in their nests; Black-throated Weavers stick blue flowers into the mud when it is still wet.

The Social Weaver of south-west Africa lives up to its name by first building a straw roof in a tree then making many chambers below where the whole colony can breed.

EGGS IN AN OVEN

We finish this review of different nesting strategies with the strangest yet simplest of all. It is used only

RSPB/D Freeman

Black-headed Weaver: one of the real 'master builders'.

by Megapodes, a group of birds found in Australia and some Pacific Islands. The eggs are laid in a hole in the sandy ground and covered up. The sun heating the sand is sufficient to hatch the eggs. Elsewhere, eggs are laid in the ground where volcanic action heats the soil. The Mallee Fowl lives in a dryer area and it also digs a pit, but covers the eggs with a mound of vegetating matter which, when moistened by rain, ferments and generates heat. The birds then adjust the heat by adding or taking away material. On hatching, their young dig their way to the surface, and are independent of their parents.

Why Did They Choose the Ones They Did?

Well, for a start, much as we would love to have had a trip to Australia or the Seychelles, unfortunately the BBC budget simply wouldn't run to it. Not that we are expensive. Heaven knows, we would probably have done it for free. Maybe we would even have chipped in a bit – but filming abroad really is a very costly operation: all those air fares and hotel bills, not to mention suntan cream and medical insurance. Anyway, it had already been decreed that this programme would be British.

In truth, though, there were a number of more positive reasons for settling on a final selection that was rather closer to home. Hilary Jeffkins explained that one of the basic principles came from a play on words. 'We wanted a very intimate feel to the pictures,' said Hilary, 'almost as if the birds were nesting *inside* the television. So birds "*on* the box", became "birds *in* the box".' In this case, a nest box.

Almost inevitably, Blue Tit was the first species chosen. It also fulfilled the other important criterion, which was to feature species that most people were already familiar with. As it happens, the public's relationship with Blue Tits probably goes beyond the level of familiarity, to surely that of a full-blown love affair. It is pretty likely that if a nationwide poll was taken to decide Britain's best loved bird the Blue Tit would win it. It's not really surprising. Not only are Blue Tits exquisitely pretty little birds – irresistible subjects for artists, who have depicted them in every medium from porcelain to postcards – but they are also full of energy and character. Even their misdemeanours – like nicking the cream off the milk – are forgiven as mischievous rather than as a nuisance. Even more endearing perhaps, Blue Tits actually seem to like human beings, almost as much as we like them. Indeed, it may well seem that they have come to depend on us to provide them with peanuts and suitable nest sites, whether they be accidental niches in our buildings, or custom-built desirable residences. And yet, no matter how well we get to know our garden Blue Tits, haven't we all wondered what actually goes on inside the nest box? Well, the BBC were about to show us. So, first choice: Blue Tit.

Second choice – again almost inevitably – Robin. Again well known, much loved and another species that readily takes to specifically designed nest boxes, which just happen to have an opening the same shape as a TV screen. A perfect bird in and on the box, if ever there was one. Mind you, Robins are also so imaginative and enterprising when it comes to choosing nest sites, that is probably the one species that really might nest inside a real television, at least, one that has been thrown on the scrap heap. As it happens, the pair we ended up featuring had a particularly novel nest to show us, but more of that soon. Meanwhile, three other species were needed for the first series.

Number three: Swallow. A bird that everyone knows, but which is nevertheless wonderfully

Swallows may return to the same beam in the same barn each year.

mysterious. Swallows arrive in spring, having made truly incredible journeys from their wintering grounds in Africa. They cross deserts, seas and mountains, returning often to exactly the same beam in the same barn where they either nested or were born the previous year. How do they achieve these amazing migrations? Well, scientists have their theories: migrant birds can navigate by the position of the sun, the moon, the stars, the earth's magnetic field, and so on . . . but, ultimately, it is a miracle. Most of us have seen Swallows zooming around the sky and skimming over a lake catching flies, but what do we know of their private lives? They don't nest inside boxes, and they are very difficult to observe. They build their mud cups up where it is cool and dark. If we stand beneath them we may just about get a glimpse of the edge of the nest – and we'll probably get spattered by the odd dollop of bird dropping for our trouble – but we can't see inside. But the BBC's cameras can. So, Swallows joined the cast.

Next, for something completely different, and yet again completely familiar. Everyone knows Kestrels. The 'motorway hawk'. While we're at it, let's just get this one out of the way once and for all. People often

RSPB/Peter Perfect

Kestrels will often take to custom-built nest boxes.

BBC./Bernard Castelein

The Kingfisher is probably Britain's most dazzling bird – and one of the most popular.

wonder whether the small birds of prey that hover over the grass verges are Kestrels or Sparrowhawks. The rule is simply this: if the bird is hovering, it is a Kestrel. Sparrowhawks don't hover. It is also true that if the birds are nesting on buildings (or even cliff faces, which are, after all, the natural versions of buildings), then they are also Kestrels. Sparrow-hawks are woodland species that nest in trees and hunt by gliding through them. The only thing that does rather confuse matters these days is that Sparrowhawks are increasingly taking to suburban gardens, so if you see a small bird of prey circling over the town, it could be either a Kestrel or a Sparrowhawk. In those circumstances, you'll need to study it and get your bird book out.

Meanwhile though . . . back to Kestrels. Fourth choice, for a number of reasons. For a start, they would provide a contrast to the smaller species already chosen. They have a different pace of life in the nest. Feeding would be less frequent, but when it did happen it would be a rather gorier affair. Kestrels are definitely not vegetarian. And how about the 'bird in a box' qualification? Pretty good actually. As it happens, Kestrels will readily take to large artificial nest boxes; or else they usually nest in holes or crevices. So, another one that would fill the

15

RSPB/Stan Craig

Little Owls do often sit out during the day, but the real action takes place after dark.

TV screen and offer a challenge to the BBC's ingenuity.

And talking of challenges . . . this led to the fifth and final choice for the first series: Kingfisher. There can't be many species that are, at the same time, so dazzlingly conspicuous and yet so difficult to see. The usual view is of a blue or orange flash – depending which side the bird is showing – as it belts away downstream at the speed of Concorde. If you are lucky enough to spot one perched, it reveals itself to be as showy as a parrot, and yet take your eye off it and you may well lose it. It is really extraordinary how that luminous plumage actually acts as camouflage amongst the reflections and dapplings of a watery habitat. The fact is, geting good pictures of a Kingfisher outside the nest is hard enough. So how on earth do you get a camera inside a nest that is at the end of a narrow tunnel, deep inside the river bank?

So that was the cast for the first series: Blue Tit, Robin, Swallow, Kestrel and Kingfisher.

The following year, for the second series, it wasn't so difficult deciding on the species. The first series had proved very popular and several of our birds had passed their live TV auditions on behalf of their respective families. So, the Blue Tits were replaced by their larger relatives the Great Tits and, continuing with the principle of a bigger (and better?) version, the Kestrels – a small falcon – were followed by Peregrines – a big falcon. An equivalent to the Robins, as representatives of garden birds, were the most numerous garden bird of them all – though not perhaps the best loved – the Starling. Fulfilling the 'how on earth did they get the cameras in there?' category, instead of the Kingfishers, we had Great Spotted Woodpeckers. And finally, guaranteeing an entirely new element for the new series, and possibly appealing to a new late-night viewing audience – Little Owls.

So that was the main cast of our avian soap opera. In theory. Those of you who followed the broadcasts will know that, as it turned out, a few other species managed to muscle in on the act. In the first series, it was a pair of Pied Wagtails and, in the second, it was Jackdaws. Here are rather fuller CVs of our principal players.

The Stars –
Profiles of Our Twelve Birds

BLUE TIT

This is the smallest and most common member of the Tit family, measuring only 11.5 cm from head to tail, which is 3 cm smaller than a House Sparrow.

With a blue top to its head, white cheeks, yellowish-green back, blue wings and tail and yellow underparts, an adult Blue Tit is almost unmistakable. Even the young are easily recognized as they resemble duller versions of their parents but with yellow cheeks.

HABITAT

The Blue Tit will be most familiar as a garden bird, but really it is a woodland species, preferring deciduous woods in central and southern Britain. It is common in lowland woods and copses throughout the rest of the British Isles.

In winter, small flocks of Blue Tits may join other small birds and roam the countryside in search of food. It is at this time that they most commonly visit gardens. If appropriate food is available, then the birds are likely to return regularly.

MIGRATION

Apart from movements into nearby countryside, there is no real migration by Blue Tits. In some years of high population in other parts of Europe, Blue Tits will move farther to new localities in their search for food and some may reach Britain.

FOOD

The Blue Tit is a very active bird and able to hang upsidedown in order to reach food. This behaviour is not for our amusement, but has evolved to help it reach food such as birch seeds which hang from the ends of thin twigs. This agility has enabled the Blue Tit to reach hanging food put out in gardens.

The chief food is insects and spiders, but the birds also eat fruit and seeds. The most important food for the young Blue Tits is caterpillars. The timing of nesting is critical because the hatch of the young needs to coincide with the maximum number of caterpillars. If caterpillars are in short supply the adults can switch to other food, but this is unlikely to be as nutritious. It has been estimated that a brood of Blue Tits consumes 15,000 caterpillars while in the nest.

NESTING

Blue Tits nest in holes, usually holes in trees, but sometimes holes in walls or other man-made objects such as street lights. They will readily take to nest boxes if they are the right size. The natural sites for nesting Blue Tits is woodland, and also in hedgerow trees. Those that choose gardens may have difficulty in finding enough food.

Broods can be large, six to sixteen eggs are laid during April or May and these hatch after 14 days. Young fly at 16–22 days but there is usually only one brood.

VOICE

The usual call is a surprisingly loud 'tsee, tsee, tsee'. The spring song is a variation on this and includes a trill.

19

ROBIN

The Robin is about the size of a Sparrow, that is to say about 14 cm from bill to tail.

Both male and female look alike, even Robins seem to have difficulty in recognizing the different sexes, but their behaviour is different and from various ritualized displays Robins do manage to work out the difference.

All adults are brown, with pale underparts and a reddish breast and face. Juveniles are brown and very spotted which gives them camouflage when they have left the nest. They moult their juvenile feathers and grow their adult plumage by their first autumn.

HABITAT

Robins live throughout the British Isles as long as there are shrubs and some undergrowth. They often live in gardens, town parks as well as woodland and farmland where there are trees and hedges. Generally they do not live in wet places.

MIGRATION

Most of our Robins are resident, but nesting pairs split up for the winter and defend separate territories. If any migration takes place it is most likely to be the females, specially young females, which move away and return the following spring. Some Robins from southern Britain may fly as far as France.

Elsewhere in Europe Robins are long-distance migrants, with northern birds moving to the Mediterranean in autumn and returning northwards in early spring.

FOOD

Typical feeding behaviour is for a Robin to watch from a low perch and to fly down to pick up an item of food. Sometimes it will hop around on the ground in its search for food, but will not usually turn over leaves like a Blackbird.

It eats a wide variety of food including the larvae of beetles and flies, small snails, worms, berries and seeds and even small fish.

NESTING

The natural nest sites are hollows in tree stumps, in an overgrown bank or among tree roots, but the Robin will readily take over an artificial site. It will use a nest box or another container lodged close to the ground such as an old kettle and even once in the skeleton of a dead cat.

Robins lay four to six eggs which hatch after 13 days. Young are in the nest for about 13 days and cared for by their parents for a further two or three weeks. There may be two or even three broods in a summer.

VOICE

The Robin is one of only a few birds which sings almost throughout the year. Its song is slower and rather sad-sounding in autumn and early winter, but early in the new year it changes to a brighter spring song. When moulting in July and August it is rarer to hear its sweet warbling song. It also has a very distinctive loud 'tic, tic' call.

21

SWALLOW

The Swallow is a small-bodied bird with longish wings, forked tail and with long tail streamers. It is larger than a House Martin; from head to tip of tail it measures about 19 cm, with males generally having longer tail streamers than females.

Swallows have blue-black backs and wings and whitish underparts. They also have dark red faces, but these can be hard to see, except at close quarters.

Young birds out of the nest resemble adults, but without tail streamers.

Flight is fast, direct and often low down, especially over water.

HABITAT

Swallows are found throughout the British Isles except the Highlands of northern Scotland and built up areas. They are most at home on lowland farmland. They visit lakes and rivers where they catch flies over the water.

MIGRATION

The return of a Swallow is often seen as a sign that summer is approaching. The birds arrive in April from their winter quarters in South Africa and they will start to return when they have finished nesting in September or October.

FOOD

Swallows have extra wide mouths for catching insects in flight. They eat flies and other insects such as aphids. When feeding young, Swallows may catch a dozen or more insects and bring them to the nestlings as a single package of food which has the technical name of a 'bolus'.

NESTING

Nests are shallow cups built up of pellets of mud and saliva and lined with straw and feathers. The traditional nest site is a barn, but presumably Swallows originally used caves or hollow trees. Today alternatives to barns are also chosen: garden sheds, garages, porches and even castle ruins are all used. Swallows do not usually nest under the eaves of houses, that is the typical site for House Martins, which are related to Swallows.

The four or five eggs hatch after 14 days. Young leave the nest at about 22 days old but depend on their parents for a further week.

VOICE

The Swallow's song is an attractive twittering and its usual call in flight is a sharp 'tswit'.

23

KESTREL

From head to tip of tail, the Kestrel is 38 cm, which is 5 cm larger than a Town Pigeon.

Males have a blue-grey head, reddish-brown back with black spots and a grey tail with a black band at the end. Underparts are cream with dark streaks. Females and young birds are less colourful with barred backs and tails.

Typically Kestrels hover in flight while hunting and this is one of the best identification points as they are the only small bird of prey to hunt in this way.

In normal flight the wings are pointed and the tail looks quite long but, if a bird soars, the wings can look broader and more rounded at the ends.

HABITAT

The Kestrel is found throughout Britain and Ireland and lives in a wide variety of habitats. It may breed in towns and cities but also nests on cliffs, crags and in trees in open countryside. It is often seen hunting beside busy roads and railway lines.

MIGRATION

Our birds are mainly resident, but Kestrels in northern Europe are migratory and some of these birds cross the North Sea and spend the winter in Britain.

FOOD

The main food is small mammals, especially voles. Kestrels also feed on insects and worms and often catch small birds, sometimes seizing them in flight, rather like a Sparrowhawk.

NESTING

Part of the Kestrel's success must be due to the variety of nest sites it uses. It will take over nests of other large birds or use cliff ledges, either inland or by the sea. Holes in trees are used and so are buildings; either old barns (like the one in the programme) or tall modern structures if there are suitable ledges or recesses. A few Kestrels nest on the ground, especially on islands where there are fewer predators.

Kestrels will also readily adopt suitable nest boxes and have been encouraged to nest in treeless areas by the provision of nest-box schemes.

They lay three to six eggs which hatch after 27 days. Young fly after about 30 days and may be looked after by their parents for a further month.

VOICE

A shrill 'kee-kee-kee'.

KINGFISHER

The Kingfisher is a small bird with a large head, big bill and short tail. It is 16.5 cm from beak-tip to tail, which is only slightly larger than a House Sparrow.

In good light, it is amazingly colourful, with chestnut-orange underparts, bright blue-green upperparts and an electric-blue rump and back which shows particularly well in flight.

Flight is fast and direct, often low over a river or lake, but sometimes over land. Because of its size and speed, Kingfishers can be surprisingly difficult to see.

HABITAT

Kingfishers live near slow-flowing rivers or lowland lakes in most parts of the British Isles except northern Scotland. The main requirements are plenty of small fish, some suitable perches to hunt from and a soft bank in which to build a nest.

MIGRATION

Our Kingfishers are mainly resident, except that they may move to the coast to escape severe winter weather, but in eastern Europe and Russia Kingfishers are long-distance migrants. There they migrate south or west to avoid the rigours of the central European winter.

FOOD

Small freshwater fish and some insects which live in water are caught by the Kingfisher diving head first from a perch or after hovering briefly. The fish is grasped in the bill, taken to a nearby perch where it is smashed several times before being eaten or being taken away to feed to the young.

NESTING

The nest site is a vertical bank close to a river or lake. The nest is in an underground chamber which is excavated at the end of a tunnel. The tunnel is usually between a half and one metre long and is dug by the parents using their feet.

In the chamber six or seven eggs are laid. Young hatch after 19 days' incubation and they fly about 27 days later. It is common for the birds to raise two broods in a season.

VOICE

The most common call is a shrill whistle which is given in flight. Once learnt, this call is usually the best method of recognizing that a Kingfisher is close by.

27

PIED WAGTAIL

A small black and white bird with a long tail, the Pied Wagtail is 18 cm from bill to tail, similar to a Chaffinch, but with a longer tail.

Males have black backs, females' backs are slightly greyer, but not as pale as the Continental version which sometimes arrives here from Europe. The White Wagtail, as the European cousin is known, has a much paler grey back and shoulders. A young Pied Wagtail out of the nest is browner with dusky underparts and a black V on its breast.

Pied Wagtails are very active and their tails continuously wag up and down as they run about.

HABITAT

A common species, which is usually associated with water, the Pied Wagtail is just as often seen well away from wet places and may visit school playgrounds, car parks and other places where there is lots of human activity. The farmyard, with water not far away, is an ideal habitat for Pied Wagtails.

MIGRATION

In northern Europe this species is a summer migrant, but in Britain and Ireland it is largely resident, although those birds in upland Scotland do tend to move south for the winter.

FOOD

The Pied Wagtail feeds almost entirely on insects which it picks up from the ground, or chases by running along the ground or by flying up and seizing the prey in the air. Pied Wagtails can hover for a few moments when hunting.

NESTING

The nest may be built in a dense bush but is more likely in a hole or crevice in a building, a natural bank . . . or even in the tool box of a tractor.

Pied Wagtails lay five or six eggs. Young hatch after 12 days and they leave the nest after about 13 days, although the parents continue feeding them for a few more days. There is often a second brood.

VOICE

The song is a warbling twittering but the most usual call is a sharp 'chis-ick' which is often heard as a Wagtail flies over with its typical bounding flight.

GREAT TIT

As the name suggests, this is the largest member of the Tit family and with vital statistics of 14 cm from bill to tail it is only a whisker smaller than a House Sparrow.

Great Tits have black heads with white cheeks, a black band down the centre of the yellow breast, a greenish back and blue-grey wings with a single white wing-bar. There are obvious white edges to the tail.

Like other Tits, Great Tits are very much at home in trees and can hang from suspended food as well as Blue Tits. They are, however, more likely to be seen feeding on the ground than other members of this family.

HABITAT

Generally Great Tits are birds of deciduous woodland and are found in most parts of the British Isles except the outer islands and some mountainous areas. Gardens are really a replacement for woodland clearings but Great Tits can be persuaded to nest if there are nest boxes or other suitable holes.

In winter the Great Tit will roam farther away from its nest site and may join flocks of other small birds which move around the local countryside, through woodlands, following hedgerows and congregating where there is a plentiful supply of food; this food supply may be a good crop of seeds, but might also be a garden bird table.

MIGRATION

Our Great Tits are not migratory and only move a limited distance from their breeding territories. In Europe some populations move farther, especially in years when populations are high or food is scarce and sometimes these birds will reach Britain.

FOOD

The most important food is insects and spiders, especially insect larvae (eg caterpillars) in summer. In winter, when insects are harder to find, seeds are eaten; particularly popular are the seeds from beech trees called beech mast.

NESTING

A hole in a tree is the normal nest site for this species, but it will also use crevices or holes in walls and other man-made sites. The birds readily take to nest boxes, and these can help to increase local populations in areas where there is a shortage of mature trees with natural holes.

The Great Tit lays three to thirteen eggs. Young hatch after 14 days and leave the nest about 18 days later. British Great Tits generally have only one brood, whereas in parts of Europe a second brood is more common.

VOICE

The Great Tit has many different calls. A loud, sharp 'tink' is often heard and the spring song is a repeating 'tea-cher, tea-cher'.

PEREGRINE

The Peregrine is the largest British Falcon, measuring 36–48 cm from head to tail. It is heavily built, the female being larger than the male.

An adult has a blue-grey back, a black head and moustache and cream underparts with fine black bars. Young birds have dark brown backs and wings, and their pale underparts have dark streaks.

Normal flight consists of powerful flaps followed by short glides. The broad, pointed wings are pulled back close to the bird's body when it swoops on its prey.

HABITAT

Peregrines need open country over which to hunt and steep rock faces, either by the sea or inland, to nest on. However, some Peregrines have found that buildings can also provide safe nest sites. A few Peregrines nest on the ground while some others nest in trees.

MIGRATION

The scientific name of *peregrinus* refers to the bird's tendency to wander. In the British Isles adults often remain in their territories all year, provided there is sufficient food, and young birds will move to estuaries or elsewhere where food is abundant. Outside of Britain and Ireland, northern populations are most likely to migrate to find food in winter.

FOOD

The Peregrine feeds on a wide variety of birds which it generally catches in the air, either by a dramatic stoop, or after a rapid chase. During a stoop the Peregrine plunges headlong with wings almost closed and strikes its prey at a speed which may reach 200 miles per hour. The victim is generally killed outright and falls to the ground, but sometimes a Peregrine will turn and seize it in the air.

NESTING

Peregrines will return to the same cliff year after year and often they use exactly the same ledge. They do not build a nest of any sort but many eyries are the old nests of other species, particularly of Ravens.

Three or four eggs are laid which hatch after 29 days. Young fly at about 35 days but they may rely on their parents for food for a further two months.

VOICE

While Peregrines are often silent they can also be very noisy as we heard frequently on the programme. We mainly heard the young shrieking for food but adults can also be noisy with their loud 'kek, kek, kek' call.

STARLING

Starlings measure 21.5 cm which is 3.5 cm smaller than a Blackbird, the only other common species with which it is likely to be confused.

Essentially a glossy black bird with spotted feathers, the Starling has a rather flat head and short tail. In flight the wings have a broad, almost triangular, base. The bill is yellow in summer but dark horn-coloured in winter.

Starlings appear far more spotted in winter than in summer, when the pale tips of the feathers actually wear away. Young Starlings are a sooty brown with pale throats and by late summer they have a strange half-adult, half-juvenile plumage.

HABITAT

Starlings are found throughout Britain and Ireland. They nest in woodland and other places where there are suitable nest sites; which may be in a village, but may also be in a town or city if there is some open ground nearby for feeding.

Once nesting is over, flocks of young join together in the countryside and large evening roosts begin to form. By autumn these roosts can number thousands of birds. Sites for roosts may be areas of dense bushes, reedbeds and, frequently, buildings in town centres.

MIGRATION

Starlings in central and Eastern Europe move out for the winter; flying south west, many arrive in Britain and swell the numbers of our own birds, most of which are resident.

FOOD

Both animal and plant food is eaten. Animal food is made up largely of insects and their larvae, including leather-jackets, which are larvae of the Crane Fly (Daddy Longlegs), which Starlings find by probing, with a half-open bill, in lawns and other areas of short grass. Plant food consists of fruit, including berries, and seeds.

Less common feeding behaviour includes riding on the backs of farm animals to pick off parasites, and engaging in aerial acrobatics in order to seize flying ants when they are swarming.

NESTING

The Starling nests in holes. Often using Wood-peckers' holes in trees, it will also nest in crevices and suitable holes in buildings. A Starling's nest is usually recognizable by the white droppings on the outside.

The four or five eggs hatch after 12 days and the young are in the nest for a further three weeks. Two broods in a summer are quite common.

VOICE

A very noisy bird which sings from prominent perches such as chimney pots and television aerials.

They have a wide range of notes and an ability to mimic other birds and animals, and even noises made by humans. The most common 'song' is made up of scratchy whistles and warbles, but it is often possible to identify other sounds such as a yapping dog, clucking chicken or chinking milk bottles.

35

GREAT SPOTTED WOODPECKER

The Great Spotted Woodpecker is 23 cm from bill to tail, 2 cm shorter than a Blackbird. It is larger than our only other black and white Woodpecker, the Lesser Spotted, which is sparrow-sized.

It has a black back with two large white patches and also white spots on the wings. The underparts are white and its head is black and white. Both sexes have crimson feathers under their tails and males also have a red patch on the back of their heads. Young birds have red on top of their heads.

Woodpeckers climb trees in a series of hops with their stiff tail feathers pushed against the tree trunk for support. They have a deeply undulating flight.

Great Spotted Woodpeckers are rarely seen on the ground.

HABITAT

Found in woods and open countryside with mature trees throughout lowland Britain, but not in Ireland, the Great Spotted Woodpecker may sometimes visit gardens and take food from bird feeders, especially in winter.

MIGRATION

This species seldom moves far from its nesting area.

FOOD

Feeds mainly on insects such as the larvae of wood-boring beetles, but this bird also eats nuts and other seeds in winter. It also frequently takes eggs and nestlings of small birds, such as Blue Tits.

Woodpeckers use their bills to chisel holes to reach insects living deep inside wood. Their very long tongues can reach inside the small chambers where the insects live. The tip of the tongue is pointed and barbed so that it can extract prey from the deepest of crevices.

NESTING

Great Spotted Woodpeckers chip out their own nest holes; the entrance hole is 5–6 cm in diameter and the nest chamber is 25–35 cm deep and 5–6 cm wide.

They lay four to seven eggs which hatch after about 12 days. Young fly 20 days later and stay with their parents for a further week.

VOICE

The most common call is a sharp 'tchack'. Instead of a song, the Woodpecker drums its bill on a branch which produces a loud resonant sound that echoes through woodland on spring mornings.

LITTLE OWL

Smallest of the British owls, the Little Owl is only 22 cm from head to tail, which is less than a centimetre larger than a Starling.

Brown with pale spots, the bird's underparts are pale with dark streaks. Its head is rather flat and its white 'eyebrows' and pale chin give it a cross expression. During the day adults will often sit out in sunlight, sometimes on very prominent perches, and will bob when curious. Its flight is often close to the ground and rises and falls as it closes its wings between flaps. The broad wings are rounded at the ends.

Male and female look alike. Young birds are covered in down when they first hatch, but by the time they leave their nest they are similar to their parents, although a little greyer.

HABITAT

The Little Owl lives on farmland and parkland with old trees in the lowlands of England, Wales and parts of southern Scotland.

In parts of Europe and the Middle East, Little Owls are found in arid areas and even on the edges of deserts.

MIGRATION

These owls are residents. There is no migration, although birds often move away from their breeding areas when nesting is over.

FOOD

Although Little Owls may be seen during the day, most of their hunting takes place at dusk or the few hours after dark and again around dawn. They will catch small mammals and sometimes birds, but most of their food is insects and earthworms. The Little Owl is the only owl to eat vegetable matter such as grass, leaves, small fruits and berries regularly.

Prey is often caught by pouncing from a perch, but Little Owls will also stalk or chase their prey on the ground.

NESTING

The most common nest site is a hole in an old tree, but Little Owls will also nest in crevices in cliffs, old buildings and even rabbit burrows. As we saw on the programme, they will adapt to suitable nest boxes.

Little Owls lay two to five eggs. Incubation takes about 27 days and the young fly after about 30 days. They are fed by parents for a further month.

VOICE

These birds have various calls of which the most frequent is a ringing 'kiew, kiew' and a yelping call. On the programme we sometimes heard a wheezing call from the young which was a hunger call to encourage the parents to go on hunting.

39

JACKDAW

The Jackdaw is the smallest of our black Crows. It measures 34 cm from bill to tail which is 12 cm smaller than a Rook and a little bigger than a Town Pigeon.

The plumage is all black except for grey on the back of the head. The eye is very pale.

Its flight is rather pigeon-like and it frequently mixes with Rooks. It is often very acrobatic in flight and frequently tumbles and rolls as if playing.

HABITAT

A common Crow which is less likely to be seen in open fields than the Rook, but also less likely to be seen in woods than the Jay. Indeed it can sometimes be seen in both places. It also likes deserted buildings, cliffs, quarries and some villages, where it is not uncommon for Jackdaws to nest in chimneys of occupied houses.

MIGRATION

There is some local migration within the British Isles. Jackdaws from bleak upland areas move to lower habitats, and other Jackdaws gather into large winter roosts. Some British birds cross the Irish sea to winter in Ireland.

FOOD

Jackdaws have a very varied diet, eating insects and spiders, fruit, seeds, dead animals and eggs of other birds. They can sometimes be seen on the backs of farm animals in their search for parasites.

NESTING

These birds nest in holes in a variety of places: in trees, rock faces or buildings and often, as we saw, they can be tempted to use nest boxes or even oil drums.

VOICE

There are two common calls of Jackdaws: either a sharp 'jac, jac', perhaps the origin of the bird's name, or a ringing 'kyow'.

How Did They Find the Nests?

Having decided on the species to be featured, it now remained to find the actual nests. Now, on the face of it, this might not seem too difficult. The BBC, after all, does have access to just about everyone in Britain. A couple of appeals tagged on to the end of the nightly television news bulletins, or scattered between records on the *Terry Wogan Show* would no doubt have brought in an avalanche of information. Add to this the fact that such groups as the RSPB and the British Trust for Ornithology are constantly monitoring and studying breeding birds, and you might well assume that locating nests of even the less common species would be pretty easy. Well, yes . . . except that the chosen nests would have to meet several qualifications.

First of all, they had to be relatively close to Bristol, which is where the Natural History Unit is based. To have had nests scattered all over the country, sending in live pictures, would have required a technical set-up that would have rivalled the complexity and expense of covering the various events at the Olympic games. Such expenditure has to be justified by very large viewing figures. *Bird in the Nest* was expected to attract a big audience, but not *that* big. The budgets and costs involved in nationwide live broadcasting are extremely complicated and probably best left to BBC accountants to understand and worry about. Also, the technical complexities are pretty mind boggling. Suffice it to say that it is not simply a matter of pointing a camera, and showing the pictures on the telly. The image has to be transmitted across the country, via a series of masts, BBC premises or satellite dishes. The simple rule is

that the longer the distances and the more 'hops' involved, the more expensive the whole process.

Not that the Bristol-based set-up was without its problems. The pictures still had to be transmitted from the particular nest site to the studio back at headquarters. This requires clear 'lines of sight'. The analogy with a cell phone isn't a bad one. Anyone who has used a mobile will know how much the signal varies. If you are on a train and go through a tunnel, the phone simply won't work at all. If you are driving, and drop down into a valley, the line suddenly fades and dies. You can imagine the problem if you were attempting to make a call from inside a Blue Tit's nest box, or from the end of a Kingfisher's tunnel! Well that's where the cameras were.

So how do we get that picture out of the nest? First, it has to go into a travelling studio, which is either in a control van parked near to the nest, or has possibly been set up in a garage or garden shed, if the owners don't mind sacrificing them. Then the signal gets sent out by a satellite dish. This looks like a larger version of a domestic satellite TV dish. In the case of a live broadcast set-up, the dish is usually positioned nearby, as high up on a hill as possible, so as to achieve one of these clear lines of sight. However, if there is no convenient natural high point, it is sometimes necessary for the dish to be hoisted way up in the air on top of a crane. What's more, that crane is mounted on a hefty lorry. Are you beginning to get the picture – to coin a phrase?

So, to qualify for the programme, the nest has to be fairly close to Bristol, in a site where you can send

A BBC invasion. The chosen nests had to have a convenient car park nearby!

BBC/Ben Osborne

out a clear picture signal and which can provide parking for a mobile studio and a big lorry with a crane and a satellite dish on it, not to mention our Birdmobile, which is yet another van, in which the presenters watch the live pictures and commentate to the nation.

Firstly, it is essential that the nest itself is accessible enough to be able to get cameras and lights into it. Oddly though, this is perhaps the least insurmountable of the problems (and, yes, we will tell you how it's done, very soon). Equally important, however, is that the nest is at the right stage to be entertaining, as it were. What do we mean by that? Well, think about it: we have a week's live broadcasts to fill. The dates are absolutely set. They appear in *Radio Times*. They can't be changed. It is no good setting up cameras and satellite dishes if, when the week arrives, the nestlings have just flown and there's nothing to see. So, nests can be 'too late'. Or they can be 'too early'. In which case, the bird just spends the whole

BIRDS NESTS WANTED!

"Bird in the Nest" is back!
From <u>Monday 29th May to Sunday 4th June</u>
BBC will be broadcasting LIVE from various birds nests.

DO YOU KNOW OF ANY NEST?

This year we are looking for the following:
1. Woodpeckers
2. Starlings
3. Great tits
4. Peregrine Falcons
5. Little owls
6. A nest in a funny place!

If you know of any such nests in your area and would like them to be filmed, please contact the <u>"Bird in the Nest Office"</u> at BBC Bristol Natural History Unit.

Telephone: 01179732211 Ext. 42208

time sitting on eggs. Not exactly riveting viewing. Or maybe it can be. As it turned out, our Kestrels did exactly that in the first series, and still provided us with some fascinating action, albeit that most of it went on outside the nest. Anyway, the point is that, ideally, each nest will have youngsters, at various stages, to provide a variety of behaviour, which will be at their best one hopes during the week they are featured on the telly.

So, it's not quite so easy as it might seem. And the question remains: how did we actually find the ideal nests? Well, the BBC put up a 'wanted' poster. For the first series it was a touch less stylish than the one for the second, shown on page 44, but equally effective. The posters were put in post offices, published in local newspapers and, along with appeals on local radio, and word of mouth amongst birdwatchers and the public, a considerable number of likely nests were tracked down. It was then up to the *Bird in the Nest* team of researchers to check them out. Many failed to meet the criteria. Generally, people were immensely enthusiastic about the idea of 'their' birds becoming TV stars, although one or two baulked at the idea of their front drives becoming BBC car parks for a week. In a few instances, it was the neighbours who complained that they had no wish to have the view from their bedroom window blocked by a thirty-foot crane with a giant satellite dish on it. Who could blame them? Sadly though, it was mainly the birds themselves that lacked the essential qualities. Some had managed to build nests where even the BBC Natural History Unit couldn't film them. Others has mistimed their egg laying, so that they were due to hatch in the week after the broadcasts; or they already had young so fully feathered that they'd almost certainly hop out of the nest the day before the programmes started. Either way, they had to be rejected, which probably didn't bother the birds much but invariably saddened their attendant humans. The researchers had to harden their hearts to the looks of disappointment on the faces of people when they were told that their nests hadn't made it.

Despite the considerable response, it was perhaps surprising how few nests turned out to be ideal. For the first series, there were plenty of Blue Tits in boxes, but even the chosen pair provided a last-minute drama, as we shall soon relate. There was, in fact, only one Robin's nest at the right stage, as it were; and the chosen Kestrel wasn't ideal, as it sat on eggs that might or might not hatch during the week. It was the same with the Starlings in the second series. Other nests, however, were exactly how the researchers would have wished them. Or – to put it another way, and to tell the truth – they were a tribute to the hard work and expertise of the people whose job it was to check them out. As I think any TV producer would agree, a series is only as good as its research team. *Bird in the Nest* has the best.

Scores of satellite dishes, miles of cables and a lot of technicians were needed to carry the pictures into your homes.

BBC/Ben Osborne

Bill Oddie

An empty garage is soon transformed into a temporary studio.

The Natural History Unit also has the best camera and sound technicians, probably in the world. The next stage of the operation belonged to them and, of course, to the birds.

Setting Up the Cameras

It surely goes without saying – though we're saying it again now – that setting up cameras and lights for nest filming (or videoing or stills photography) is the most delicate of operations. It requires immense skill and care and an exact knowledge of the bird's behaviour and habits. In truth, birds' tolerance of human activity varies from species to species. Not surprisingly, garden birds – such as Robins and Blue Tits – will put up with more disturbance than, for example, the ultra-sensitive and secretive Kingfishers. Equally, even within the same species, some individuals will be more nervous than others. New, 'first year' parents tend to be edgier than more experienced breeders. In all instances, it is probably true to say that it is during the period when the birds are incubating eggs that they are most prone to abandoning the nest, and extra caution is in order. Once the young are hatched, the instinct to go on feeding them is very strong, and this sometimes allows the cameramen to take what might appear to be extraordinary liberties. However, techniques that might be acceptable to a Blue Tit would not be tolerated by a Kingfisher. We repeat, nest photography is a job for the expert. None comes more expert than the BBC Natural History Unit. So please leave it to them, and don't try this at home.

The exterior camera outside the Blue Tit's nest box on the BBC-issue garden shed.

BLUE TITS

It all seemed so easy. The house was in the rural outskirts of Bristol. Detached, in its own grounds and, frankly, in a pretty sumptuous setting. There was a wide drive and even a sort of a spare car park for all the unit vehicles. It was also up on a hill so that there were no problems sending out the signal. Best of all though, was the garden. The family were extremely 'bird friendly', and every tree had been fitted out with a nest box. What's more, several of them were in use. There was a family of Great Tits in one, and families of Blue Tits in two others. We even had a choice. Surely this was the ideal set up. Nothing could possibly go wrong. Oh no?

About a week before broadcasts were due to begin it was as if a curse fell upon the place. Suddenly the weather turned cold and wet. Such conditions immediately put an extra strain on parent birds who are feeding hungry chicks. If the nestlings are very young and without the natural insulation of feathers, then they will require extra brooding to keep them warm. Meanwhile, the supply of insect food – which is their staple diet at this stage – will be harder to find. Caterpillars and spiders don't relish getting cold and wet any more than the birds, so they tend to hide. Mind you, when the weather is warm, they tend to get eaten more readily, so it's not much of a life either way. Prolonged spells of cold wet weather can actually prove fatal for young birds in the nest, but a short inclement snap is usually surmountable: as long as there are two healthy parents to share the duties. Unfortunately, in our apparently ideal garden, no sooner did the bad weather strike, than so did a local moggy. A cat killed one of the adult Great Tits. The single remaining parent simply couldn't brood and collect food at the same time and the chicks starved to death.

True, the Blue Tits were our chosen species, but the signs were ominous. They rapidly became worse, when one of the Blue Tits' nests was raided and the whole family disappeared. This time, tell-tale gnawing round the nest-box hole suggested that the murderer had been a Grey Squirrel. Clearly this garden was by no means the safe haven that it had at first appeared. It was rapidly becoming the garden of death. Moreover, time was getting short. It was essential that the lights and cameras be set up, as this process has to be done carefully by stages, so that the birds have time to get used to the equipment. But the immediate priority was to make sure that we didn't lose our stars before they'd even appeared on the screen, or – perhaps even worse – during their first broadcasts. A decision was made to make the remaining nest box predator proof. First though, it had to be moved to a more manageable position. The fact was that this remaining box was located high up on the trunk of a tree, where the squirrels could get at it but our cameras couldn't.

The manoeuvre that followed may well seem extraordinary. The fact that it was entirely successful is testament to the devotion that Blue Tits have to feeding their families and to the knowledge and experience of the BBC team in knowing what the birds will tolerate. The first step was to take the box down from the tree and reposition it on the side of a garden shed. It was the work of but a few minutes, during which time the parents carried on collecting caterpillars or perched nearby watching curiously. Just to make doubly sure that the chicks didn't become chilled they were kept warm with a 'hand warmer'. As soon as the box had been relocated, the adults carried on feeding their family in their new position, showing absolutely no surprise or puzzlement. Which was more than could be said for the owners of the house, who arrived home that evening to find a brand new garden shed in the middle of their lawn. This was BBC issue and in effect, a wooden hide. But before the cameras and lights could be introduced, the nest box had to be made safe.

So, having allowed the birds a few more feeds, the reinforcement team set to work. First, they provided a metal plate on the front of the box that would seriously bend the teeth of any squirrel that attempted to gnaw at it. Then, they added a section of wire netting 'baffle', to prevent any would-be intruders from climbing up and sticking their paws inside. Finally,

they moved the shed even farther into the middle of the lawn, as far away as possible from any cover that would allow predators to creep up unobserved. Once more, the Blue Tits showed their appreciation by carrying on feeding their family as if nothing had changed. Did they know they were safer? And did they know they were being watched?

Well, they were. Because inside the garden shed was not a lawn mower and piles of plant pots but a tripod and a remote control camera. The lens was

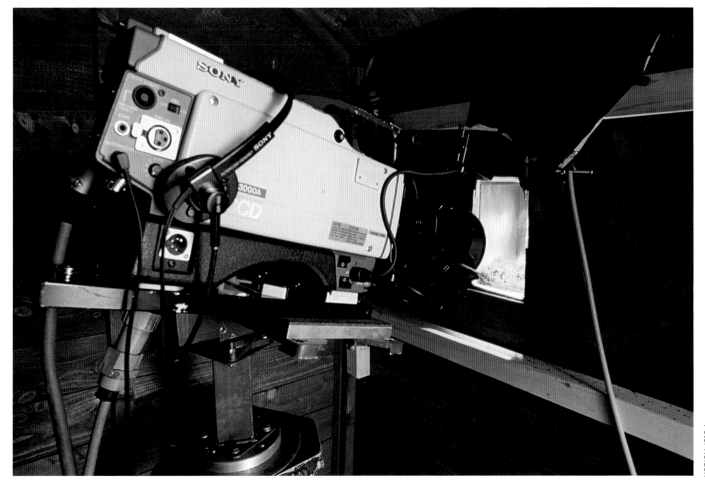

The interior camera, showing us what goes on inside the Blue Tit's nest box. The glass back makes it look like a little stage!

Peter Holden

pointing towards where the back of the nest box was attached to the shed. The back wall of the box itself had been removed and replaced with a glass panel, thus allowing the camera to see what was actually happening inside the box. However, the pictures would be very murky as at this point, since the only light entering was through the tiny hole in the nest box. To illuminate the situation further therefore, a small lamp was set up inside the shed. The light was not suddenly switched on, which could startle the birds (though it probably wouldn't have frightened them away). Instead though, thanks to a dimmer switch, the picture gradually became brighter and clearer. Meanwhile, the Blue Tits simply carried on as normal. They didn't even pause to pose in the spotlight, or smile at the camera. What was immediately obvious was that feeding hungry nestlings allows no time whatsoever for distractions.

In addition to the camera and light, a small microphone picked up the squeaking of the baby birds. Another camera, set up outside in the garden, pointed at the nest box and recorded the movements of the adult birds as they came and went. It would also eventually – we hoped – capture the moment when the chicks took their first peek at the outside world, and their first flight.

This then was the basic arrangement which applied to several of our nests: a camera taking pictures of inside the nest, a microphone to pick up sound and, if necessary, lights to improve the picture; plus a second camera following the happenings outside and around the nest site. There were, in fact, considerable variations on this theme amongst the various species but, as it happened, the Blue Tit-type set-up applied equally successfully in the second series to the Great Tits.

GREAT TITS

The Great Tits' nest box was also moved from a tree on to a nice new BBC garden shed, complete with remote control camera. Most of the cameras, by the way, were remote control. There was, in fact, room for a cameraman to go inside the shed but it was only necessary occasionally to do so to check the lighting or to clean the glass. Otherwise, the camera was fixed on a tripod, pointing at the nest, and operations such as focusing and zooming in or out – to give close ups or wider shots – were all controlled from inside the nearby mobile studio. Not only did this mean less disturbance for the birds but it also saved a few cameramen from stiff necks and aching backs (it wasn't a very big shed).

The Great Tits' box was – rather like the Blue Tits' – situated in a splendid garden, next to a splendid house, which would have had a splendid view, if it hadn't been obliterated by the enormous BBC vehicles. The owner – bemused rather than upset – did claim that he hadn't realized there would be quite so many vans, cars and lorries, but the reward of seeing his Great Tits on the telly seemed to be ample compensation. Moreover, the birds fledged soon after the week's broadcasts, so the disruption was pretty short lived. Which is more than could be said for that caused by our Robins.

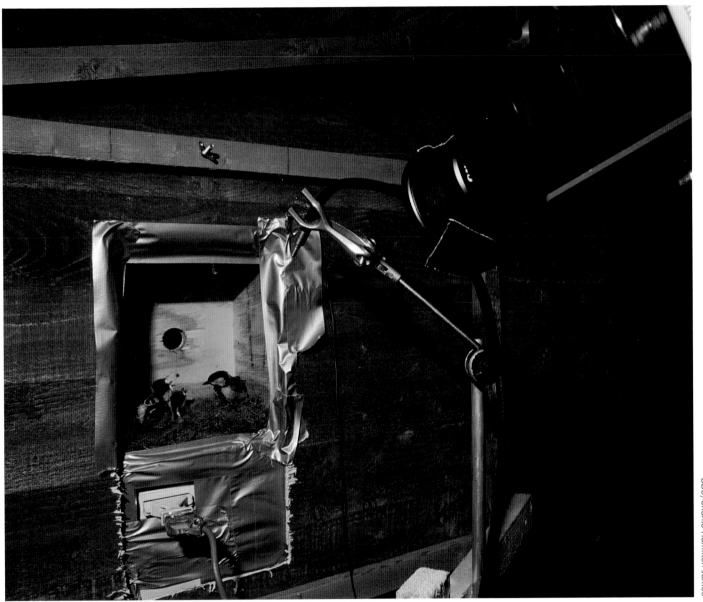

The Great Tit's nest box, on another BBC shed, with room for camera, lights and, occasionally, a person.

ROBINS

Robins are famous for nesting in strange places and in peculiar objects. Maybe they are into recycling or something but they do seem more than willing to raise their families in just about anything thrown away that has nest space in it. Empty paint tins, rusty buckets, old boots and, of course, discarded kettles all seem to attract Robins the second they are chucked out. It almost seems like justification for throwing scrap around the place – but it isn't. On the other hand, a few such objects purposely placed around the garden are excellent nest-box substitutes. Robins will, of course, also use 'proper' nest boxes, as long as they have Robin-type rectangular entrances (not the Tit-box-with-a-hole type). In the absence of such artificial sites, crevices in rocks, walls and trees are equally suitable. In short, Robins are pretty adaptable, and any well-used mature garden habitat will offer them lots of places to nest. As indeed did the suburban garden on the outskirts of Bristol that was the home of the *Bird in the Nest* Robins of the first series. Yes, it was ideal Robinsville. Lots of old walls, gnarled trees, thick hedges, garden sheds (real weathered ones, not put there by the BBC). In short, masses of nest sites, all ignored by our Robins, who chose the outside toilet.

They just got there in time. The house owners were in the process of rebuilding part of the back of their property. A certain amount of demolition had gone on, now there were cement mixers and piles of bricks lying around and they were no doubt anxious to get on with the more positive construction part. But not so fast – the Robins had other ideas. At some point during the building (or knocking down), the window to the outside toilet had been slightly broken. It wasn't a big hole and it was rather jagged and nasty looking. But that didn't stop the Robins. In fact, they probably thought it made it even better. What predator would risk gashing its paws on broken glass? And what a paradise that sharp-edged little hole led to. Warm and safe, a handy perch on a toilet roll holder, and a snug little ledge to build the nest on. And so they moved in.

The house owners were faced with a dilemma for

The outside toilet occupied by Robins. They go in through the jagged hole in the window. Ouch!

Peter Holden

Robins in the convenience clearly meant an inconvenience for them. But they did the right thing. All building work was suspended and the toilet was declared 'engaged' until the Robins chose to declare it vacant again.

Not only was the site perfect for the Robins, it was pretty much ideal for the *Bird in the Nest* crew as well. Plenty of room for the lights, microphone, and remote control camera. (Mind you, I do hope they remembered to remove them after the birds had flown and people started using the loo again. Could be a bit embarrassing.)

As it happens, the reason this particular nest was chosen was not because of its novel setting – honestly! The truth is that it was, genuinely, the only Robin's nest that had been reported that would be at the right stage during the week of the programme. In fact, it was ideal. The house owner had been keeping an eye on the eggs and we knew, within a day or two, when they were due to hatch. There was, indeed, a very good chance that this would happen live during the early broadcasts. Just to make absolutely sure that the happy event would be captured on video though, the team had got the camera ready and in position a day or two early. A good thing too, as it turned out. The day before the series was due to start, the eggs did indeed begin to crack. Not to worry, we had a camera. Unfortunately, though, we didn't have any tape in it . . . The producer received a desperate and somewhat profane call: 'Quick send a tape . . . the blighters are hatching!' (Well, it wasn't actually 'blighters' but it did end in 'ers'.) Happily, the tape arrived and so did the baby Robins, some of them during the first day's broadcasts.

BBC/Ben Osborne

The Robin's nest on the ledge – dangerously close to the loo!

SWALLOWS

Bob runs a traditional farm not far from Bristol. Visiting it really does remind you how prolific and important such places can be for wildlife. Sadly, it also highlights how barren modern farmland tends to be: no hedgerows, no grassy margins, huge fields of the same crops sprayed with chemicals. The consequence is: no wild flowers, no seeds, no insects, no food, no nesting places, and hardly any birds. In contrast, at Bob's place, we were spoilt for choice. What's more, since Bob is himself a bird-watcher – and indeed a qualified ringer – he knew the exact locations of the nests, how long they'd had eggs, or how old the chicks were. All we had to do was place our order. 'We'd like a Swallow's nest please.' No problem, there were half a dozen to choose from in Bob's splendid old-fashioned barns. 'And we'd like a family of youngsters old enough to be getting ready to fledge by the end of the week.' 'Certainly, that's the one you want.'

The nest was perched half way along a beam, up in a dark corner. The main problem would be where to put the camera so as to be able to see into the nest. The lens would also need to be up on a beam, ideally slightly higher than the nest. It really didn't look as if there would be room for the relatively large video cameras that were being used on the Robins or the Tits. This was a job for modern technology. So, in came the 'pencil' camera. It really is pencil sized (and not a particularly big pencil at that). Along with it, came an equally tiny fibre-optic light. It looked barely more than a brilliantly bright spot – a 'pin source', they call it – but it provides all the illumination that the camera requires. Both light and camera are attached to the end of a bendy 'antenna'. This is the same kind of incredible miniaturized technology that is used to do internal scans in medical work. It really can go in anywhere. Suffice it to say that it gave us simply stunning pictures of our Swallow family.

A second camera, this time with a quick-reflexed real live cameraman, was positioned outside the barn. His job was to follow the adult birds as they zoomed in and out carrying food. He occasionally also went roving round the farm, understandably unable to resist picking up pictures of some of the other residents. In particular he couldn't resist the Pied Wagtails.

The Swallow's nest is on one beam, the miniature camera on another.

RSPB/Roger Wilmshurst

PIED WAGTAILS

They weren't mean to be in the series but they just had to be included. They had built a nest in a little niche on one of Bob's tractors. Not an old broken-down tractor. One that was still in use. In the early days, while the female incubated her eggs, Bob literally took her for a ride once or twice a day. Being a bird expert, he was able to judge when hatching time was nigh and, perhaps fearing the chicks might be experiencing a bit of tractor-sickness inside their shells, he switched to another vehicle, and let them settle in one place to raise the family. A camera was set up near the nest and, with a splendid sense of timing, the new chicks greeted the world and a few million viewers on live television.

We would clearly have to return to Bob's farm for the second series. Ironically, however, the results were not quite so captivating. It wasn't that there weren't just as many birds to choose from. There were, again, plenty of Swallows (but we'd done them) and there were House Martins near by, and more Pied Wagtails (or maybe the same ones but, rather more conventionally this year, nesting in a hole in a wall). Unfortunately, though, we chose Starlings.

The Pied Wagtail nest on Bob's tractor.

Peter Holden

STARLINGS

Starlings tend to get rather a bad press. Actually, it surely depends how you look at them. Some people complain about their vast flocks messing up town centres. Others find the same flocks absolutely spectacular, as they wheel around like magically co-ordinated clouds. Some people can't stand the Starling's 'song': 'just a jumble of noisy twittering'. Others are intrigued by their amazing ability to mimic everything from other birds, to wolf whistles and telephones. Then again, some might find them kind of boring to look at: 'just sort of black, aren't they?' On the other hand, if you see one in bright sunlight, you might be dazzled by the iridescent plumage, reflecting all colours of the rainbow. Are they ugly or characterful? Quarrelsome or full of energy? Well, maybe it was a desire to do a good PR job for the species that made the *Bird in the Nest* team vote for Starling for the second series.

Alas, the birds did not return the compliment. The main problem was that there simply weren't any nests at all that seemed to be at the right stage. There had been a warm spell in March and April, and most of the Starlings had got off to an early start. The result was that, by late May when the series was due to begin, no matter how many wanted posters were put up and radio appeals and phone calls made, the researchers simply couldn't find a single nest with chicks in it. First broods had fledged long ago – in fact, the fields at Bob's farm were full of the khaki-brown youngsters – and it seemed that adults weren't ready to try for a second brood for a while yet. Except one.

The only Starling nest available was under the eaves of the village hall, close to Bob's place. It contained four eggs, but we didn't know how long they had been there. There was no choice though but to rig up a camera. It was a cramped space, so it required the same type of miniature gear that had recorded the Swallows. There was no problem getting pictures. But there *was* a problem with the Starlings. Several times we went over live, only to see what might as well have been a still photograph of the eggs. No bird. No movement. A pretty colour, yes, nice sky blue, but not exactly thrilling telly. Once or twice, a bird did pop in – presumably the female – and sort of prod the eggs with her beak. Then she'd disappear again. She didn't even sit on them for more than the odd minute, and that rarely when she was 'on the air'. There were several theories. Maybe the eggs were addled and as she suspected it, she wasn't prepared to waste time incubating them. Or maybe she was the neglected wife of a bigamous male and was finding the whole business a bit dispiriting. Or maybe it was so warm under the eaves that she didn't need to sit on the eggs to keep them warm. Perhaps it was sort of a natural incubator in there. Whatever the truth though, one thing was becoming clear. This particular Starling – or its eggs – were definitely not going to become TV stars.

It was time to give the understudies a chance.

JACKDAWS

'Bless farmer Bob,' is all we could say. In a masterly display of recycling – with a touch of irony – he had collected old oil drums, emptied and cleaned them, and then strapped them high on the trunks of a row of trees, where they had instantly become Jackdaw nest boxes. The technical team didn't have time to set up anything very elaborate but they shifted the miniature camera and lights from the Starlings and transferred them to inside the Jackdaws' oil drum, rapidly and efficiently enough for the Jackdaws to take their place as an officially featured species for the rest of the second series. To be honest though, they weren't all that much better than the Starlings. There were two youngsters in the nest. They did have enormous white-rimmed mouths which gaped open a bit like Rod Hull's Emu whilst they were being fed, and the momentary effect was pretty photogenic. But not for long. Unfortunately, the Jackdaw's feeding regime is fairly leisurely and, most of the time, the chicks lay fast asleep. At such times, the picture was less than lively: two black birds, inside a black oil drum. Oh well, you can't win 'em all!

The Jackdaw's oil barrel nest box, courtesy of Farmer Bob.

Bill Oddie

KESTRELS

The Kestrels required a major construction job. We had been shown the nest by another bird-friendly landowner. It was in a small rectangular hole, at the very top of a wall, in a big brick barn. Exactly what the hole was for, we weren't quite sure. Maybe there had once been a very small window up there, but why? Or perhaps it had been a ventilation grill. Or maybe a pulley used to go through it to pull sacks of grain up and down to a balcony that had long since disappeared. In any event, what it was now was an ideal nesting cavity for a pair of Kestrels. Apart from being snug, dark and peaceful, it was also almost inaccessible. There weren't any convenient beams or windowsills nearby on which a camera could rest – what was needed was a nearby tower. Even then, the camera would be inside, looking out through the Kestrels' space, and the only source of light was the bright sunlight streaming in through the nest entrance. This would mean that any birds in the nest would appear merely as black silhouettes. Thus, the tower would have to also accommodate a certain amount of lighting, plus, of course, a microphone. It was going to have to be quite a big tower, and strong. So the team set to work with a pile of scaffolding.

This would have been fine if the tower was not being built next to a Kestrels' nest. Birds of prey are nervous by nature, far less tolerant of disturbance than Blue Tits or Robins. To make matters even trickier, our pair included a particularly edgy and inexperienced young female, who was apt to take fright at the slightest noise.

Have you ever tried using scaffolding quietly? Just stand by a construction site for a few minutes and you'll hear what I mean. You only have to breathe on an iron pole for it to clank, and the noise is magnified like a church bell down the hollow metal. Building the scaffolding tower took a lot of care, patience and time. Every time the bird left the eggs for a few minutes, the team rushed in with nuts and bolts and tried to add on a couple more feet. A look-out, outside the barn, warned the workers that she was about to return, at which point they had to down tools, hide behind the hay bales, staying there till she went for another fly round when they could carry on.

The scaffolding tower had to be built quickly and quietly while the Kestrel was off the nest. Not easy.

Peter Holden

Eventually though, the tower was finished, complete with its camera, microphone and lights. In addition, the back of the nest was fitted with a little black velvet curtain, to screen off the technical paraphernalia from the nervous bird. Unfortunately, every now and then, the cloth would begin to come away from its moorings and start flapping around, rather like the hem of Dracula's cloak. Amazingly, this didn't seem to panic the Kestrel as much as the producer, who felt that it spoilt the picture. It probably terrified some of the children watching as well.

Geoff Vian with his roving camera at the Kestrel site. He managed to capture all sorts of action.

As always, the *Bird in the Nest* team triumphed and we got some great pictures. We saw both male and female incubating the eggs (which proved once and for all that they do share the work, despite what some Kestrel experts had told us). When pictures of the bird falling asleep on its eggs became a bit too soporific, we were able to cut outside to where a roving cameraman was picking up all sorts of action: the male bringing in food to a 'plucking post', where it defeathered its prey; the female coming to get her lunch; other passing wildlife, such as Buzzards and Rabbits; and lurking predators, like egg-hunting Crows, who were noisily seen off by the Kestrels.

We also saw quite a lot of people. Ironically, considering that the birds were so nervous, they had chosen a nest site that looked down on a rather busy little road. It was fairly noisy, especially after turning-out time at the local pub. Nevertheless, they would have probably remained largely undetected had it not been for the fact that they were about to be featured on the telly. A giant satellite dish and a mobile studio, full of expensive equipment, tends to attract public curiosity at best and a small criminal element at worst. Since the site was so close to the road, it was necessary to keep a 24-hour watch on it, to make sure nothing was stolen or vandalized. At least this meant that the birds and their nest were also being permanently guarded. However, this didn't prevent people wandering past and stopping outside the barn, pointing up at the nest site, and calling to their friends: 'Oi, come and have a look. There's Kestrels up in there, you know.' Actually, there usually weren't because they'd been scared away by the voices. Fortunately though, they always came back, although one night it was after dark before the female returned and we all got very worried. It really brought home to us how vulnerable some birds are to human interference.

PEREGRINES

Peregrines have several enemies. All of them human. They have been shot, and poisoned by man's pesticides. Their eggs are often stolen, either by collectors or by illegal bird traders who try to hatch them, then rear the young to be sold to equally illegal falconers. Such people will also take young Peregrines from the nest. (Falconry itself is not illegal but the birds must be bred in captivity.) It wasn't long ago that Peregrines were becoming very rare birds in Britain. Fortunately, thanks to tighter laws, better enforcement and careful conservation, this truly magnificent bird has made quite a spectacular comeback in recent years. And anyone who has seen a Peregrine in the wild would surely agree that they are spectacular. The *Bird in the Nest* team was equally convinced that

Peter Holden

The Peregrine's habitat: wild and apparently inaccessible – but not to BBC cameramen.

they would look magnificent on the television and would surely inspire people to support their protection.

It was clear, however, that because of the sensitive nature of the species, we would have to keep the location of the chosen nest site as much a mystery as possible. Ironically, this isn't easy, since Peregrines are so admired that local people – and not just bird-watchers – tend to regard 'their' Peregrines as something of a tourist attraction. Most of the eyries are well known and, indeed, much visited. This is, in fact, no bad thing, since it means the birds are under constant vigilance and this deters the criminals. To be honest, the Peregrines featured in the second series of *Bird in the Nest* were very well known indeed. Nevertheless, we never once actually told the viewing public where they were. And we're not saying now either!

In any case, whether or not you recognized the narrow ledge on the huge cliff face, I'm sure you'd agree that it must have taken a brave man to have got a camera up there. The Natural History Unit have to have mountaineering skills as well. The nest was nearly half way up a sheer precipice that was over three hundred feet high. So, dangling on ropes with crampons, the team constructed a small scaffolding 'buttress' which housed the main camera. It was, of course, remote control. It really would have been a bit too much to expect a cameraman to stay strapped up there for a week. The whole thing was then covered in camouflaged cloth. Looking up at the nest site, it was extremely hard to spot. Even the cable snaking down the cliff was lost amongst the vertical crevices. Certainly the set-up was a great deal less conspicuous than the birds themselves. The Peregrines tended to be pretty noisy on the ledge – they no doubt felt completely safe up there.

As well as the nest camera, a second camera was set up on the other side of the 'canyon'. This was fitted with a very strong telephoto lens and was able to offer a different view of the eyrie, even though it was barely visible through binoculars from so far away. The second camera also picked up some wonderful action as the adults soared overhead, brought food into their 'larder', or just sat preening and posing. The pictures were surely a magnificent advert for the species. Seeing these wonderfully wild birds it was hard to believe that anyone would want to harm them.

Ian Stacy mans the camera on the other side of the gorge, filming the nest through a very powerful lens – whatever the weather.

BBC/Charlie Hamilton James

LITTLE OWLS

Our Little Owls came to us courtesy of the Ministry of Defence. They lived on a part of Salisbury Plain that is regularly used for military exercises but is also the domain of Major Lewis, who has managed single-handed to increase vastly the number of breeding birds in an area that was pretty prolific in the first place.

Meanwhile, back to our Little Owls, arguably the stars on the second series of *Bird in the Nest*. Owls are, in fact, birds of prey, but the contrast to the Peregrines, or indeed the Kestrels, could hardly be greater. For a start, reaching the nest did not need quite such a head for heights, or such an elaborate construction. A small ladder was all that was required to climb up to the nest box, which was fixed on an ordinary-looking tree. Not that the nest box was ordinary. Just as Farmer Bob enjoyed the irony of using oil drums to provide protection for wildlife rather than problems, so Major Lewis no doubt appreciated the recycling of ammunition boxes to provide homes for one of nature's most placid and friendly birds. Yes, Little Owls might be birds of prey – and they do have sharp little beaks and talons – but, at close quarters, they are as cute as Muppets. And calm and gentle with it. Setting up their camera required, firstly, lifting the lid of the ammunition nest box. Inside it, was as peaceful a domestic scene as you could ever wish to see: four little ball-of-fluff babies, being cuddled by their mother. She merely blinked her big yellow eyes as the old lid was replaced by a rather thicker new one, packed with the miniature camera, light and microphone. She didn't even move.

At the base of the tree was a large crate containing the control gear. A turn of a knob slowly brought up the brightness of the fibre-optic light and, for the first time, we saw live pictures from inside a Little Owl's nest. In truth, during the daytime, not a lot happened. They just snoozed away, looking lovely. But then Owls *are* nocturnal. Well, believe me, their first night was so full of action that it deserves its own chapter (see pages 85–8).

Like most of our nest set-ups, there was also a camera covering the comings and goings outside the box. However, it soon became apparent that the only shot it was likely to get was of an adult flapping away in silhouette, as darkness fell and the hunting began. By the time the real action was under way, it was pitch black out there. But the BBC have ways of dealing with these things. In this case, it was an infra-red camera, which was soon installed and giving us fantastic pictures of the parent birds bringing food into the nest and of the chicks peering out. Magical stuff.

One ex-Army ammunition box, Little Owls for the use of!

Bill Oddie

Battery

Light

Camera

KINGFISHERS

Certainly this was the most elaborate and difficult set-up from a technical point of view, requiring incredible expertise. Well, they don't come more expert that Simon King: cameraman and naturalist, and a bringer of wildlife 'hot shots'. (Which just happens to be the title of one of Simon's TV series, in which he explains how he gets some of his astonishing pictures.) Simon is also a Kingfisher expert. There was never much doubt then that it would be one of 'his' nests that would be featured in *Bird in the Nest*.

It is impossible to exaggerate how tricky a job this was. Kingfishers, despite their gaudy colours, are shy, sensitive birds, easily disturbed or discouraged. They also have a very specialized lifestyle that must not be disrupted. Added to this, they nest in what might seem truly inaccessible places: they excavate a tunnel into the side of a river bank. The tunnel is narrow (just big enough for the birds to go in and out) and it is quite long (up to a metre). At the end of the tunnel is a slightly larger chamber, where the eggs are laid and the young are reared. It is also, of course, pitch dark in there. So, how do you get live pictures from inside a Kingfisher's nest?

Very slowly, is the first answer. About a week before broadcasts were due to start, Simon – and Charlie, his assistant at this site – began digging a pit into the top of the river bank, alongside the tunnel. They worked behind a canvas screen, so that no movement was visible. During this time, the Kingfishers were coming back and forth to the nest, feeding what were very recently hatched young. It was essential that they were not aware of any human presence. Simon only dug whilst the birds were away catching fish. Charlie kept watch – or rather he kept listening. As soon as he heard the thin 'peep' call of a returning adult, he warned Simon and Simon stopped digging. It took the whole week to dig a big enough pit. It wasn't huge, but it had to accommodate a camera (not a miniature one in this case), fibre-optic lights and, for a while, Simon himself. For although Simon would not be operating the camera from in there, he did have to make the final break through to the nesting chamber. To do this, he had to have room to operate. An operation was exactly what it was like. First, he had to measure how far down the bank the entrance was to the tunnel. Then, he had to estimate how long the tunnel was. Then, he began very, very carefully, using a spoon and fingers, to scrape away the earth inside the wall of the pit alongside the nest chamber. Think of it as a miniature version of *The Great Escape*. Only this time, you're trying to get *into* the cell. Of course, the closer he got to the chamber, the more delicate the work had to be. Probably the first evidence that he'd got through was the smell – the fishy stink of rotting Sticklebacks that are the Kingfishers' staple diet. They can be quite messy eaters.

Once through, Simon had to work very fast indeed. Baby Kingfishers are not covered in fluffy down like, for example, the Little Owls. For many days they are blind and naked. Although it must be pretty warm and fetid in their black hole they still have to be brooded constantly by their parents or they will catch chill and die. They must not be subjected to draughts. So, the first thing Simon had to do was fit a small glass panel over the hole where he had broken into the chamber. This then had to be carefully sealed, so as to be absolutely draught-proof. Next, the camera was fixed on its tripod, so that the lens was looking through the glass and into the nest. Then, it should be able to get pictures of the babies. But it was absolutely pitch dark in there. The only light was a very faint glow of daylight coming from the tunnel entrance some way away. So, it was another job for the amazing fibre-optics. Again though, it had to be taken slowly. The intensity of the light was increased gradually, so that it did not alarm the birds.

At last, on our screens back in the studio, we were able to see what the camera was seeing: unique pictures of very young Kingfishers, looking incredibly primitive, positively prehistoric, almost like tiny Pterodactyls. At this age, they can't see, they have no feathers, and they hardly move. But they do defecate! Usually, they do this instinctively towards the mouth of the tunnel, towards the light. Now, however, they had a new light to react to. So, they squitted all over the glass, thus obliterating the picture. Which was another reason the pit had to be big enough for a man to get inside: to wipe the window . . .

The incredible task seemed to have been achieved successfully. Meanwhile, a second camera had been set up outside to follow the adult birds on their fishing trips. Ironically, it was the early pictures from this camera that began to worry Simon. He soon noticed that the pair seemed unevenly matched. The female was catching her quota but she was paired with an inexperienced male who really didn't seem to be much of a fisherman. Young birds are very hungry. They require constant nourishment, as well as brooding by the female. Supply and demand have to be equally matched. In this case it wasn't happening. Simon felt that the chicks were already suffering from an inadequate food supply. The evidence suggested that, with a male as incompetent as this, the female might well not be able to cope, and the youngsters would probably not survive. It is not common practice for wildlife film makers to interfere but, in this case, it seemed justified. Simon set up a fish tank in the river nearby which every now and then was replenished with a supply of tiddlers. The male remained unenterprising but the resourceful – and wiser? – female soon got the idea and helped herself to the fast food. So did the chicks, who rapidly began to look healthier. Well, as healthy as blind, naked Kingfisher chicks ever do look. So, human involvement can be good, or bad. So far, so good.

GREAT SPOTTED WOODPECKERS

This nest not only introduced us to one of our favourite birds but also to our favourite human: Enid. Enid's garden is a veritable sanctuary. Birds love it. Enid loves the birds and it's pretty likely that they love her. There are plenty of them: Tits, Robins, Blackbirds, Thrushes, Finches and so on and all the facilities they could desire: feeders, bird tables, a little pond and lots of lovely plants and bushes for food

and nesting. There is also a tree, right in the middle of the lawn. The *Bird in the Nest* team didn't actually put it there but they could well have designed it. The tree was only about seven or eight feet high, and about two-thirds of the way up the trunk was a hole. Inside the hole, was the nest of a pair of Great Spotted Woodpeckers.

Enid knew them well. She had christened them Woody and Winnie. When Enid saw the BBC's 'wanted' poster, she rang the Natural History Unit. The researchers who came to check out the nest really couldn't believe their luck. The site had everything:

The tent around the Woodpecker tree containing lights and camera.

BBC/Charlie Hamilton James

66

there was an empty garage, in which to set up the mobile studio and an empty drive next door, where they could park the Birdmobile and the satellite dish. Enid's kitchen had a big window, from which they could survey the garden, while dining on a supply of tea and buns. And most incredible of all – there was that nest.

The thing is, Great Spotted Woodpeckers may be the most garden friendly of our British Woodpeckers and they do indeed often visit feeders in winter, *but* they usually nest deep in woodland, at the top of very tall, difficult-to-climb trees. They *don't* usually nest five foot off the ground in the middle of suburban lawns. Our method of setting up the camera was similar to that for the Kingfishers but much, much easier. Instead of digging delicately with a spoon, the tool required here was a large electric saw. A Woodpecker's 'chamber' is sort of a woody equivalent of the Kingfisher's tunnel, except that it is vertical and by no means as deep. But it is still quite dark in there and it was still going to need a glass panel at the back if a camera was to see inside. Hence the saw. Displaying an impressively delicate touch, our worker sliced off a sliver of wood from the back of the tree to expose the nest and the chicks therein. This was immediately covered by a draught-proof panel, so that the youngsters didn't catch a chill. Then, a canvas hide was attached to the back of the tree (rather like a square-shaped tent). There was room in there for a normal-sized camera on its tripod, the usual lights and sound equipment and for a man, when necessary, whose first job was to replace the panel with a glass window. The same principle as for the Kingfishers, or indeed the Tits.

The whole operation went perfectly to plan. Enid was delighted. So were we. Winnie seemed perfectly happy too. Alas, Woody was in no position to

join in the celebrations, but that's another story. . . . Coming soon (see pages 83–5).

The cameras were in position. So were the birds. But would it all work on the television?

Bill Oddie

Inside the tent. The camera can see through the 'window' into the Woodpecker's nest.

The Rehearsal

The great day for the launch of the first series of *Bird in the Nest* arrived. We were met in Bristol by Hilary (the producer), Roy (the director) and others from the production team; given lunch and then taken to see the *Bird in the Nest* headquarters – the control room, as it were. This was inside a large studio at the BBC's Broadcasting House in Whiteladies Road, pretty much in the middle of the city. It was immediately clear that the production team was not going to see much sunlight for the rest of the week. The studio –

The Birdmobile looking nice and new at the beginning of the week. Lots of room in there.

BBC/Charlie Hamilton James

probably once used for light entertainment shows – was enormous. It was also rather cold and gloomy. In one corner of this cavern was the *Bird in the Nest* control set-up, looking rather temporary, which in fact it was, since it would only exist for the one week of live broadcasts. There was a huddle of desks and chairs, equipment boxes, piles of plugs, cables and other electrical bits and pieces. The centrepiece was a bank of monitors: small television screens, lined up on various tables. In a proper permanent control room the monitors would be built into one wall, and the production team would have nice, sumptuous swivel chairs to sit on and a big flashy control desk, with a neat bank of buttons and switches on it. However, in this case, everything had a rather more do-it-yourself feel to it. It was a bit like the difference between purchasing a nicely integrated, colour co-ordinated, neatly built-in hi-fi set and buying all the components separately to create your own system. Hi-fi boffs prefer to do that, 'cos it's more of a challenge. In the case of the *Bird in the Nest* team, I suspect they had to make do with what was available.

Nevertheless, it all seemed to be coming together. Technicians were plugging in things, and production assistants were consulting clipboards. Someone else was sticking bits of tape on to the monitors. Each screen was labelled. Some with technical terms we didn't understand, others with bird names. Each species had its own screen: Blue Tits, Kestrels, Swallows, Robins and Kingfishers. Occasionally, an image would appear tantalizingly – Blue Tit chicks fast asleep, the hole in the window of the Robin's toilet – and then it would disappear again. At this point, the Kingfisher monitor was completely black. Was it a live picture from inside the nest or just a blank screen? Nobody seemed quite sure. In any case, we were being hustled out of the studio. We noticed that another of the monitors was labelled

'Birdmobile'. So what was that then? We were about to find out.

Half an hour later we clambered into the van that was to be our daytime home for the next six days. The inside of The Birdmobile looked like a small, cramped version of the control room back at Bristol. It certainly wasn't the customized hi-fi version. The only seats available were square box-like things that looked about as comfy as a pile of house bricks. They felt worse. After a few hours sitting on them, we reckoned house bricks would have been softer. Perched on these, we could face forward to talk to a camera, which was on a tripod just inside the door of the van, and was operated by a real cameraman, who looked about as uncomfortable as we were. In this position, we were 'in vision', which meant that we – the presenters – could actually be seen by you, the viewers. So we really should look as though we realized it. We were told that when we heard the instruction – 'Coming to you in vision' – we should face the front, and talk 'to camera'. We practised it. OK, what's next?

It was then explained that when we were given the instruction – 'Turn to monitors' – we would have to swivel round (on our non-swivelling boxes), crick our necks, and look at our TV screens. These had been set up at the back of the van, on what was probably a picnic table, now disguised by a piece of cloth. What immediately struck us was that we hadn't got as many monitors as they had back at the Bristol control room. This came as a bit of a disappointment to us. Until then, we had assumed that we would be seeing pictures from all five nests at the same time and that we would be able to decide which one we wanted to talk about. Wrong. It was explained to us that it was tricky – and expensive – enough transmitting all the pictures back to Bristol. To 'feed' them all to The Birdmobile as well would be impossible. Well, that was what they told us. Actually, we couldn't help thinking that the real reason was that the producer and director wanted to remind us that they were in charge, not us, and that we'd jolly well get what we were given. Fair enough. Presenters present. Directors direct.

In any event, this was the routine we were to follow. Each day, The Birdmobile would be parked near the site of one of our five nests. For the purpose of this Sunday rehearsal, we were alongside the Blue Tit garden. On our monitors we would be able to see the following pictures: on two of the screens there would always be – live – whatever was happening at the nest we were alongside, both inside the nest and outside. On another of the screens would be whatever the control room decided to show us. So, we would be able to see pictures from only one other nest and the producer or director would decide which one

BBC/Ben Osborne

Lots of room? Inside the Birdmobile. With two presenters, a cameraman and an assistant producer, it was not quite as comfy as we would have liked.

that would be. So, yes, we had to accept it – they were in charge. On the fourth screen was whatever was going out on television at the time. When we were actually on the air, it would, therefore, be pictures of ourselves or the birds. During the breaks, we could watch what we liked. Generally we still watched the birds, but in the first series we were occasionally diverted by some reasonably interesting Test Cricket. During the second series, this fourth screen proved a bit more of a distraction, since we coincided with the early rounds of the Rugby World Cup. It says something for the tolerance of the BBC, that they allowed us to watch ITV. As long as we didn't do it when we were 'in vision'.

Meanwhile, back on that first day – clearly we, in The Birdmobile, were going to have to follow instructions from the director, back in Bristol. So how would this work? It was too far from him to shout. We were going to have to have 'talk back'. 'Talk back' involves being 'wired up' and having a little earpiece in one ear, through which the control room can speak to the presenter. Interviewers and reporters on live news programmes have them. So, at the same time as they are reading the news or grilling a politician, they are probably being spoken to by the director, saying such things as 'Give him a hard time' or 'Ask him about his mistress' or, worst of all, just when it's getting interesting, 'You've only got five seconds left'. This explains the glazed look many TV presenters often have, or why they seem to be completely ignoring the person they are interviewing, or why they suddenly go all panicky and stop in mid-sentence. Having 'talk back' during a live broadcast is absolutely and entirely necessary. It is also a bit of a nightmare. For a start, the earpiece soon begins to hurt. Well, ours did. But then we hadn't had time to have nice, custom-built, personally moulded ones. But, whether your earpiece is snug or not, it can still

deafen and confuse you. The nastiest noise you can hear is called 'feedback'. It happens, by accident, when someone is testing microphones or has pressed the wrong button somewhere. Feedback is an excruciating high-pitched whine that threatens literally to pierce your ear drums. It can happen any time, and when it does, it is hard not to scream. You just hope it won't happen when you are live.

The major decision with talk back though, is whether you want it 'open' or 'closed'. When we were first asked this, we weren't really sure what it meant. 'Open talk back' sounded rather more sociable, so we opted for that. Wrong again. What it meant was that we could hear *everything* that was going on back in the Bristol studio. This included, not only the director giving us directions, but also the producer discussing the next part of the broadcasts, the technicians saying technical things, the tea lady asking if they wanted sugar, a secretary sobbing about an unfaithful boyfriend, passing fire engines and police sirens, and extraneous users of the airwaves, that varied from mini-cab firms to the speaking clock. We very soon realized that that way madness lay, and that we preferred our talk back 'closed'. Closed talk back meant that the only voices we heard from Bristol were the ones we were meant to hear.

We rehearsed the communication process. The director gave us instructions. The production assistant gave us countdowns. And the producer gave us encouragement. Well, that's how it was meant to be. We practised a theoretical model sequence. All we would hear in our earpieces – on closed talk back – would be such things as: 'Coming to you in 10 seconds ... 5 ... 4 ... 3 ... 2 ...1.' and 'You're in vision ... now.' We would then talk to the camera a bit, until we were told 'Turn to monitors ... and going to Blue Tits.' We'd then discuss the live pictures of the Blue Tits till we were told 'OK . . . there's a feed at the Swallows. Go to Swallows.' At which point, one of us would say something like 'Ah, look there's action at the Swallows,' and the picture would change. And so it would continue, until we neared the end of the broadcast, at which point we would hear in our earpiece a calm voice telling us: 'Thirty seconds left . . . wind up now, please . . . 20 . . . 10 . . . 9 . . . 8 . . . etc.' During which, we would, totally unruffled, sign off and invite the viewers to join us again soon, finishing speaking just as we heard the signature tune and director telling us, 'And that's the end of the broadcast' and the producer adding a cheery 'Well done!'

Well, that was the theory. As it happened, theory was about all we got during that first afternoon. Time ran out before we could do a proper rehearsal. And, in any case, not all the cameras were transmitting yet, as technicians all over the West Country wrestled with cables and satellite dishes and so on.

Nevertheless, we saw quite enough to be encouraged and extremely excited. Before we had to finish for the day, we did achieve a quick whip round all the nests. And there they all were. Live pictures from all five. Even the Kingfishers. That really was an historic moment. It was still murky in the chamber at the end of their tunnel. The fibre-optic light hadn't been turned fully on yet. But the camera was working. And there they unmistakably were. Four weird looking little creatures, with their mother shielding them with her wing. The iridescent blue hardly registered in the gloom. But she was there, and so were they. And so were we all. It was probably at that moment that all of us on *Bird in the Nest* became convinced that this really was going to be something special.

That evening everyone was nervous. It was a bit like anticipating taking part in a major sporting event the next day. What we needed was a good night's sleep.

Peter Holden

The nice, peaceful hotel that the BBC put us in. Thanks.

Nesting Time –
the Climax of a Bird's Year

During the programmes we were asked many questions about the different ways in which birds nest and look after their young. In this chapter we will try to explain some basic biology to help explain many of the pictures we were seeing on our screens.

The birds which are nesting are those that survived the winter, and also some that survived the stresses of a long migratory flight from Africa; now all their energy is directed at breeding, because they need to reproduce in order for the species to continue. But breeding brings its own difficulties and its own dangers.

WHY DO MOST BIRDS NEST IN THE SPRING?

Because breeding is difficult and dangerous, birds must choose the best time to nest. A plentiful food supply is vitally important; there needs to be maximum food to give their offspring the best chance to survive. There is no point in waiting for a glut of food before starting to nest, because the food may not still be there when the young need it most, therefore preparations need to start early.

FINDING THE RIGHT PLACE

Once a male bird has reached breeding age it needs to establish its own territory. Jackdaws, being sociable birds, live in colonies and only defend a very small territory around their nest. Peregrines, on the other hand, will defend a large area, perhaps a quarter of a mile or more, around their nest and they hunt over an even greater area.

Finding a territory can be difficult for a young bird in its first year. Older birds have all the advantages. The only chance for a young male is to find a territory where the owner has died or to try to squeeze a small territory between larger ones; if there is plenty of food for all then he may be able to expand his territory.

WHAT MAKES A GOOD TERRITORY?

There does need to be plenty of food for the female to maintain sufficient energy to lay her eggs. For example, the weight of a clutch of Blue Tit's eggs, laid over ten days, is more than the total weight of a female Blue Tit. Obviously she needs a good supply of food to make that possible. The male can help by feeding his mate in a display known as courtship feeding.

KEEPING A TERRITORY

Having found a territory is not enough, that territory needs to be defended against others of the same species. Fights are rare and for many small birds their songs are the chief method of showing a territory is occupied. Other species use special signals called displays and some use both song and display.

Our Peregrines, for example, would have been displaying and calling three months before we joined them on their cliff ledge. Their display involves variations on hunting behaviour and both birds would have stooped and dived around the cliffs where they later nested. This would mainly have been courtship, but it would also have indicated to other Peregrines that the territory was occupied.

Our Great Tits may have formed a pair during the winter, or the male may have returned first. His 'teacher' song would have indicated the territory was occupied and he would have had three displays to chase off any competitors: first, he would display his yellow breast with its broad black stripe; second, he would spread his wings and point his bill at the enemy; third, he would show his yellow and black

BBC/Thomas D Mangelsen

A Peregrine in its element.

RSPB/W S Paton

breast and then make a number of short flights round the rival.

Great Tit. The most desirable males have the widest breast stripes. Apparently size does make a difference.

HOW DO BIRDS ATTRACT A MATE?

Once a territory is established by a lone male, then a female must be attracted to it. Sometimes a pair will arrive together, or both birds from the previous year will return to the same site. But if one has not survived then a new pair needs to be established.

Quite how pairs form is still not understood. There

is some evidence that female Great Tits will choose males with larger black stripes on their bellies. It also appears that these male Great Tits are larger, stronger and make better parents. Even the quality of a bird's song may influence the choice of partner: experiments have shown that it is the Sedge Warblers which have the longest, most complicated song that attract females first.

WHICH BIRD CHOOSES THE SITE AND MAKES THE NEST?

Once a territory is occupied and a mate attracted, the nest site needs to be selected very carefully. In Chapter 3 we looked at the wide variety of sites that are used by birds. What all the sites have in common is a means of protection for the eggs and young and proximity to a supply of food for the whole family.

Our male Great Tit will have selected several suitable holes and the female chosen the best, she will then have used it as a roost for several days or even weeks (which is a good way of testing it) before she builds her nest of moss lined with hair or fur. The male takes no part in the nest building. Blue Tits have a similar arrangement, but when it comes to lining the nest the Blue Tit is more likely to use feathers.

With Jackdaws, Swallows and Great Spotted Woodpeckers, both male and female will have shared the work of building the nest. For the Swallows, the amount of work will have depended on how much mud could be found in the vicinity of the nest. For the Woodpeckers, the entrance hole and nest chamber would be excavated during early spring and defended from Starlings which often take over Woodpecker holes.

The construction of the Kingfisher's hole was another great feat. The male may have done most of the digging, but it is likely that both birds played a part. The soil would have been loosened with their bills and then dug out with their feet. It takes the birds between one and two weeks to dig a tunnel of a half-metre or more with a nesting chamber at the end.

The female Robin does all the building and her nest of leaves, straw and grasses takes about four days to construct. A pair of Pied Wagtails seem to share the duty of nest building, with the male doing most of the early work and the female finishing off.

The male Starling can't seem to get it right. He starts to build the nest but soon the female takes over. When completed, the male then often brings in leaves and flowers to decorate the nest but these are often thrown out by the female.

Peregrines often use traditional sites and build no nest at all; we do not know which bird chooses which ledge to use. Neither do we really know how Kestrels make their choice but it seems likely that the male selects several possible places and the female then makes the final decision. With Little Owls we have no idea how the nest site is selected, but it is the female which scratches out the debris before laying her eggs.

WHEN ARE THE EGGS LAID?

Once the site is chosen and the nest built then the eggs are laid. Most small birds lay an egg a day, but with larger birds, such as the Peregrine, there may be a two- or three-day gap.

The trigger for laying is critical for birds like the Great Tit which needs to coincide the fledging of its young with the largest number of caterpillars. Temperature in March and April is important but not the whole story. Just how these Tits predict when the maximum number of caterpillars will be available is still a mystery to us.

WHY ARE THE YOUNG USUALLY THE SAME AGE?

Most birds wait until the clutch of eggs is complete before starting to incubate. This ensures that all the eggs will hatch at about the same time. The main exceptions are some birds of prey which start incubation from the time the first egg is laid and therefore have quite different hatching dates for their young. As it happens the Peregrine doesn't do this; it waits for the clutch to be almost complete before incubation starts. And looking at the size of our four young Little Owls it would seem certain that they also all hatched at about the same time.

RSPB/E A James

Young Starlings. The khaki plumage will have been moulted to black by autumn.

WHY DO SOME BIRDS HAVE MANY MORE EGGS THAN OTHERS?

The size of the clutch varies with the species, it also varies with individuals. As we saw earlier, the Peregrine may have only three or four eggs while the Blue Tit may have as many as sixteen. Also, the Robin may have four to six eggs, but it may also have two or three broods in a summer, whereas Peregrines and Blue Tits will only nest once.

Small birds whose young develop quickly will often have more than one brood provided there is food available. Robins can continue to find food for their young throughout the summer but the Blue Tit, which depends on caterpillars, has only a short season before its prey pupates or is eaten by other birds.

The number of young reared is not only linked to food, but also to the chances of survival. Small birds such as Robins and Tits are very vulnerable, almost half of the adults die each year. Food shortages and poor weather, both when the young leave the nest and during the following autumn and winter, and number of natural predators (not to mention cats) combine to ensure that fewer than one in five will survive until next spring. In addition, there is a greater likelihood of a whole nest being wiped out by a predator, whereas the Peregrines at the top of the food chain have only humans as their enemy and are long lived once they have learnt to hunt success- fully.

Bill Oddie

Barn Owl chicks. Notice the huge difference in size. The smallest may not survive – it could even end up as a meal for the others.

Highs and Lows

THE KINGFISHERS' STORY

The day didn't start well. For reasons we never did discover, we had been given a dodgy map. Every morning during the week's live broadcasts, we were driven from our hotel in Bristol to the site of whichever nest was to be featured on that particular day. Tuesday – the second day of broadcasts – was Kingfisher Day. The Kingfisher nest was along a river bank, not far from a bridge, in a part of the West Country that seemed to have little else in it except river banks and bridges. For nearly two hours, we did a frantic tour of the wrong bridges and banks. Even when we thought we were approaching the right place, we found our way blocked by a ford. We were pretty sure that the site was only a hundred yards away over the other side but nearby fishermen assured us that the water was far too deep to allow our car to get across. So we had to take the long way round.

By the time we got there, it was ten minutes after we should have been on air for our first live broadcast of the day. We'd missed it. This was particularly upsetting, as we had got very excited about our Kingfishers. On the previous day, we had seen live pictures from inside the chamber at the end of their tunnel and they really were astonishing. Neither of us had anticipated just how primitive the youngsters would look. They were more like little reptiles: blind, naked, except for the beginnings of the feathers which, at that early stage, are sort of clingfilm wrapped inside a membrane – the official term is 'in

pin', because the shafts resemble little more than pins. What had definitely struck us was that the chicks looked incredibly vulnerable and fragile but they were being well fed from Simon's submerged tank.

So we really had been looking forward to that first broadcast. When we finally did arrive at the right place, we were a mixture of apologetic and cross.

'We're really sorry. We've been driving around the area for nearly two hours! The map was wrong. Where did that map come from anyway?' we protested.

'It's OK,' we were reassured, 'Simon did it.'

At which point, Simon King appeared from behind The Birdmobile. We now switched to a mixture of apology, crossness and gratitude. We were also a little envious. Simon is an experienced presenter – he'd probably made a better job of it than us. But, even as we relaxed and began to make light of the incident, we began to sense that all was not well. Have you ever been in one of those awful situations when you suddenly realize that the comment you've made is in very bad taste? Or when you are grumbling about something relatively trivial and someone else breaks some really bad news. You feel awful. Yes? Well . . . it was about to happen to us. Even as we wittered on about dodgy maps and uncrossable fords, Simon interrupted us:

'You know what's happened, don't you?'

'No. What?'

'The baby Kingfishers are all dead.'

The news stunned all of us. It also upset the viewers. For the rest of the week, and indeed long after the series ended, we continued to receive calls and letters saying how distressed people were. Several times during what should have been a really exhilarating day, we had to tell the story. This is what had happened.

The final live broadcast of the previous evening had been fairly late. Only an hour or so before dark. Simon had been watching, and no doubt anticipating enjoying the pictures for which he could take a great deal of the credit. However, what he saw rang alarm bells. The chicks were alone. They were not being brooded, despite the fact that the light was starting to fail and the air beginning to chill. Moreover, the nestlings were shivering. In fact, young Kingfishers do often tremble and, since they are also blind and naked, to be honest, to an inexpert eye, they don't look exactly bursting with health and energy at the best of times. But Simon's eye is very expert indeed. He recognized immediately that the babies were stressed and possibly neglected. He leapt into his car and raced to the site. Fortunately, he knew exactly how to get there, and quickly.

What he discovered was a most alarming and completely unpredictable scenario. There were cars parked all along the narrow road that ran closely parallel to the river. And there were people all over the place. Some were consulting maps, others were rushing up and down rummaging in the foliage along the river bank. There was lots of chattering and laughter, as they searched for clues. A Treasure Hunt was in full swing. Every now and then, among the noise, Simon could hear the distant anxiety calls of adult Kingfishers. The disturbance was a disaster. If the female had already been in her tunnel when the invasion had begun, she might well have stayed put and it would have been all right. Unfortunately though, she had been caught out of the nest, probably on the last fishing trip of the evening. There was no way

that she would return while there were people constantly rushing backwards and forwards up and down the river bank.

Simon, and other members of the BBC team, tried to control the treasure hunters and reason with them. 'There are definitely no clues along this stretch of the river,' they assured them, 'please leave.'

Frankly, the responses were mixed. Some people co-operated and either left or kept quiet. Others refused. 'This is our fun, you're not going to spoil it,' seemed to be the attitude.

Pleas for the Kingfishers fell on deaf ears. It is possible that, had the incident occurred later in the week, more people might have known about the birds and they would have behaved more sympathetically. As it was, it's likely that the treasure hunters must have felt pretty embarrassed, if not downright guilty, when the result of their activities was broadcast to the nation the next day.

The consequences were fatal. It wasn't till after dark that the female felt safe enough to return to the nest. At this point, the chicks were certainly still alive but they had been deprived of food and warmth for so long that they did not survive the night. One can only imagine the helplessness Simon must have felt when he saw the first pictures the next morning. Ironically, 'live' had become 'dead'.

Everyone was upset, and indeed angry. On the other hand, we couldn't help reflecting that this sort of unwitting and unintentional disturbance must go on all the time. We only happened to know about this particular incident because we were broadcasting from that site. Nevertheless, it was very upsetting. Once we human beings become involved with particular birds – individuals or families – we simply can't help grieving for them almost as deeply as we

The Kingfisher arrives back at the nest after a successful fishing trip. Everything seemed to be going so well.

would for fellow humans. However, it would be a mistake to assume that the birds themselves feel these things equally deeply. Certainly many species have 'anxiety calls'. Robins and Blackbirds, for example, utter undeniably mournful whistles when their chicks have been taken by predators. But the wake is short lived. And so it was with the Kingfishers. It was a strange contrast on the river bank for the rest of that day. The weather was gorgeous, but the *Bird in the Nest* team hardly basked in it. Instead, we just sat there, sad and silent. There was one noise nearby, however: the piping of a pair of Kingfishers, as they sped up and down the river, displaying to each other, and preparing to try again.

THE WOODPECKERS' STORY

As we've already said, everything in the Woodpeckers' garden seemed lovely. It was idyllic for birds and humans alike. Woody and Winnie's nest in the middle of the lawn. The BBC's camera in its hide. The studio in the garage, and Enid in her kitchen. Arguably, the only thing that added a slightly sour note was the fact that to get into the garden you had to cross a rather busy road, with a wicked curve on it that, instead of slowing drivers down, seemed to tempt them into pretending they were in a Grand Prix. It was a perilous crossing for people. For a certain Woodpecker it proved fatal.

Only a day or two before broadcasts were due to begin, a male Great Spotted Woodpecker was brought into Enid's house. Apparently, it had flown low across the road and straight into a passing vehicle. Probably the bird never knew what hit him, and maybe neither did the driver. As it turned out, ironically, it had not been one of the local boy racers, but a lorry driver who, on learning about the tragedy when watching *Bird in the Nest*, was so upset that he came and confessed. He had to be reassured that it really wasn't his fault. In fact, the bird was not killed by the impact but it was clearly badly stunned. It wasn't, of course, absolutely certain that the bird was Woody, but it seemed likely and subsequent events surely confirmed that it was. Warmth, tender loving care – and probably the kiss of life and a few prayers as well – were duly administered and, by the evening, the Woodpecker seemed recovered enough to be released in a nearby tree. Sadly though, he was never seen again. It was just possible that it hadn't been Woody at all, and that it had flown off back to its territory. Another optimistic, yet rather cynical,

theory suggested that it *was* Woody but that he might have been a bigamist with two wives, and that this incident had forced him to make a choice. Or maybe he'd just figured that this breeding business was far too dangerous and he was off to seek a quieter life. The more realistic verdict was: 'missing, presumed dead'. In any event, for all practical purposes, Winnie was now a widow and a single parent.

This was a crisis. The eggs were hatching and the four chicks were very small. Rather like the Kingfishers, which they closely resembled, they were unfeathered and helpless. They needed not only feeding but also brooding. Normally Woodpecker pairs share these duties, and indeed it is arguable that two parents are necessary to successfully bring up a family. Would Winnie be able to cope on her own? Or should we help her?

It was a hard decision. A producer with a cynical eye on the ratings could more or less have guaranteed a heart-rending drama in the avian soap opera by allowing nature to take its course, even if it involved the loss of some or all of the youngsters. In

Bill Oddie

'Beware! Woodpeckers crossing.' Alas too late.

Winnie Woodpecker. A single parent's work is never done.

BBC/Charlie Hamilton James

subsequent days, they were, on the advice of the bird dieticians at the British Trust for Ornithology, supplemented with waxworms (slightly bigger and squishier, and full of goodness for young Woodpeckers). This menu and regime prove entirely successful and the chicks grew rapidly. Every now and then, the food supply was withdrawn for a while, just to make sure that Winnie didn't become so dependent and lazy that she'd forget how to catch her own grubs.

The only snag here was that it seemed that the best natural food supply was in the local orchard: on the other side of that busy road. Several times we saw Winnie swoop precariously low in front of passing traffic. More BBC enterprise was called for. In no time at all, a fence of soft green netting was erected along one side of the garden, tall enough to force Winnie to make her crossings at a slightly higher altitude. Above lorry height, anyway. A couple of times she actually bounced in and out of the screen, but she soon got the idea.

All in all, it was a very satisfying tale. During the week, Winnie and her family entranced the viewers, as well as our team, and Enid, who kept a caring eye on everyone – birds and humans. Not many days after the live programmes, the four youngsters began to leave the nest. Their departure was captured on video, but only just. They chose a BBC breakfast break to pop out and Lloyd (the on-site guardian) had to stand with his hand over the hole while the cameraman raced back from the local café. He made it before they starting pecking through Lloyd's fingers and Winnie's happy ending became one of the highlights of the update programme a few weeks later.

The only sad note was the never-forgotten Woody. For one rather surreal moment, we thought we'd found him. In the middle of the week, the Television

human 'soaps', writers spend hours with black coffee thinking up such plot lines. But the *Bird in the Nest* team is made of softer stuff, we're delighted to say. It was decided to give Winnie a helping hand. Or rather several large helpings of mealworms. These were placed, at regular intervals, in a smart little perspex dish, just below the nest hole. This meant that she only had to dangle down a few inches to fill her beak, before swivelling round to pop back in and feed her babies. She could also afford the time to brood them, knowing that she'd never have to be away long looking for food. Winnie was already well used to nibbling at Enid's peanuts, so she was no stranger to accepting 'artificial food'. Not that mealworms, which look like dry wiggly maggots, could really be classed as anything but natural. On

We put up this safety net to make sure that Winnie didn't go the same way as Woody.

News carried pictures from Cape Kennedy in Florida, where a Woodpecker was delaying the launch of a space shuttle by hammering holes in the NASA spacecraft. Maybe Woody had acquired a taste for telly, flown across the Atlantic and was making a bid for international stardom. Or perhaps there is a sort of worldwide jungle telegraph amongst these birds – that drumming does carry an awful long way. Had they decided it was 'World Woodpecker Week'? Well, such whimsical thoughts keep you chuckling when you're stuck in The Birdmobile for hours on end.

The truth was, of course, much less glamorous. When the crew were finally clearing up the cables and cameras in Enid's garden, they found what was left of Woody under some thick bushes. He had no doubt died of internal injuries after the crash. At least

his children were alive and well and zooming around the garden at that very moment. We just hoped Winnie was teaching them the Green Cross Code.

THE OWLS' FIRST NIGHT

One ex-army ammunition box, Little Owls for the use of, supplied by Major Lewis of the Hawk and Owl Trust. This nest really was something special. And so were the birds. They had already enchanted us during their first daytime broadcast, even though they hadn't done much except huddle together and look sweet. This is, of course, what owls – both adults and

the live monitor, literally erupted into action. First one adult, then another, squeezed inside. The chicks suddenly scampered forward as if they'd been wound up by clockwork, as they grabbed at the worms and moths that had been brought in. Then almost as quickly as they'd come, the parents were out again. Then they were back, with more moths. There was probably a hatch of moths close to the nest and the birds were grabbing all they could while the supply lasted. Water birds sometimes go into the same sort of frantic action when there is a shoal of fish to be plundered. It is sometimes referred to as a 'feeding frenzy', a pretty appropriate expression. Our Owls were tazzing around so quickly that it really did look as though someone was playing the video at double speed. But, no, this was happening live.

Even when a feed wasn't in progress, the chicks were tremendously active. They always seemed to be rearranging themselves. Cuddling up in different formations, preening one another, or scratching and flapping. At one point, it looked as if they'd caught the spirit of the Rugby World Cup, which was in progress at the time, as all four youngsters huddled up into a scrum and went for a push-over try. Then one of them started a backward digging movement with one of his claws. Was he trying to heel the ball back? Probably he was instinctively trying to gouge out a cosy hollow to lie in. Unfortunately, no one had told him that Major Lewis's ammunition boxes had hard floors.

As we watched, it began to strike us that it was rather appropriate that these birds were on army property. It really did look as if some of the young Owls' manoeuvres had been drilled with military precision. After each feed, they would change places and line up neatly again, as if they were expecting kit inspection. In fact, what they were doing was making sure everyone got an equal share. The one aspect the

chicks – tend to do during much of the daylight hours. That's their sleepy time. Dusk is when the action begins. We certainly weren't going to miss it.

In fact, it was rather a grotty sort of evening. Dull, damp and chilly. We were grateful that for once we were being allowed back at the headquarters in Bristol, which, for the second series, was much cosier than during the first. This year, the control room was tucked neatly into an executives' boardroom, rather than an enormous studio. Apparently, the executives weren't entirely pleased at being ousted but it is to be hoped that they came to realize that it was for a very good cause. Certainly, we were pleased to be indoors on such an inclement night. What's more, we were able to share our excitement with the rest of the production team in person, rather than simply hear their distant voices on our earpieces.

It was at about half past nine when the adult Little Owls left the box and flapped off into the night to go hunting. The outside camera captured their ghostly silhouettes. Back in the box, the chicks huddled patiently together. A few minutes passed, then suddenly the inside of the nest box, and the picture on major might not have been so pleased about was the deteriorating state of the nest, which was rapidly becoming strewn with moths' wings and bits of worms.

'Come on, you 'orrible Little Owls, get this place tidied up!'

'Look at the state of that plumage. Get those feathers preened, you scruffy lot. At the double!'

This really was going to be fun. Between us we practised a 'major voice' and checked up our Owl facts, while the birds continued to perform. The broadcast was due at ten past eleven. If it was anything like as entertaining as the rehearsal, it would be a beauty. Half an hour to go. Keep it up, you lovely Little Owls.

Suddenly there was a lull. Then, a drama. Before our very eyes, one of the chicks shuffled over to the nest box exit. He poked his head out. All we could now see of him was a fluffy bum. Then – ignoring our cries of 'No! Come back' – he disappeared. The exit led into a small 'corridor', which in turn led to the hole at the front of the box. Outside that, was the big, big world and the dark, dark night. Minutes

passed. The chick didn't return. The other three sat in a corner, suddenly quiet, as if they were thinking, 'Where on earth has he gone to?' We all began to get worried. Perhaps more so, when an adult returned and fed the other three but failed to push the wanderer back into the box. Was he still out in the corridor? Or had he fallen out of the tree and on to the ground below? If so, he was certainly in danger from any passing Fox, or even a larger Owl. Then we got a call from Lloyd. He was actually out on Salisbury Plain, keeping an eye on the nest from not too far away. Except that the night was so dark that he really couldn't see anything of it. But he could hear. What he told us was even more worrying:

'I can hear a distress call of a young Little Owl. I've only heard that sound when they are being picked up.' For example, in the jaws of a predator? This was awful: the first night, and one of our adorable little babies goes and commits suicide.

Suddenly one of the production assistants gave us hope. She was listening to the live nest sound on earphones. The tiny, but·very sensitive microphone, secreted in the box lid, would pick up the slightest noise.

'I'm sure I can hear scratching,' she announced. 'Shhhh!'

Everyone in the control room fell silent, as we strained our ears. Was it really scratching, or just the wind rattling the branches? Yes? No. Yes.

With only a couple of minutes to go before he was due on the air, the wayward chick reappeared at the hole and scuttled back to join his siblings. The whole team cheered!

The Owls' First Night was – to coin a phrase – a real hoot. They captured the hearts of all who'd stayed up to see them and they carried on that way all week. We soon realized that the errant chick had merely been using his initiative to try to jump the queue, by intercepting the returning adult out in the corridor. At first, we worried that he might get unfair preference, and the other three be neglected. But no way. True to their intelligent nature, the Owls had it all sorted out. Several times, mum or dad squeezed past the queue jumper, even though he almost blocked the entrance making it a very tight fit, and a very amusing piece of live action. Then the other chicks caught on to the routine and, displaying a discipline that would surely delight Major Lewis, they took it in turns to be first out in the corridor. As they grew bigger, they all ended up out there at feeding time, thus saving the adults the bother of coming right inside. Clever birds, and born TV stars. It was particularly gratifying to be able to thank them at

close quarters, as we were able to do before they left their nest.

ROBINS IN THE LOO

Actors call it 'corpsing': getting the giggles, when you're supposed to be serious. Probably you've seen clips on *It'll be All Right on the Night* or *Auntie's Bloomers*. Of course, the straighter the face you're meant to keep, the more embarrassing it is, and the funnier it is to watch. It's particularly entertaining to see a newsreader or a particularly pompous thespian in the middle of a Shakespearean soliloquy trying to

control themselves. Of course, the television viewers don't usually get the chance to revel in such fun, because most programmes are recorded. On a recorded programme you can afford to get the giggles and it doesn't really matter too much, because you know you can do another take. Mind you, if you do too many takes, the director is likely to get a bit cross with you, as it wastes time and money. And if it is you that is corpsing you feel like a naughty schoolboy being told off by teacher for giggling in class. Sometimes though, even the boss enjoys watching performers finding it absolutely impossible to get their lines out without laughing. However, if this sort of thing happens on live television you are in real trouble. And *Bird in the Nest* was live. Both of us would have to confess to being inveterate gigglers. The evidence is on video.

The Robins nesting in the outside toilet were always going to be a potential problem. Be honest, the set-up was a bit silly. Every time one of us explained to the viewers where the nest was, we were aware of a tiny catch in our voices, which was a telltale sign that we were having to suppress a little chuckle. In fact, a little chuckle would probably have been OK, but the problem is that, under the nervous stress of live performance, a little chuckle tends to grow rapidly into a full-blown giggling fit. Nevertheless, for the first few days, we kept straight faces and steady voices.

Then we got a letter. It came from a concerned viewer. It actually made a perfectly serious point:

'Dear *Bird in the Nest*. I am becoming increasingly worried about the Robins nesting in the outside toilet. I can't help noticing that the lid is up. Is there not a danger that the birds will fall in?'

A good point, and one which we felt we had to discuss and indeed answer on the television, as other viewers may well have had the same concern. We

rehearsed our answer. We thought it actually unlikely that the adult Robins would fall down the loo, unless they fancied a quick dip, in which case, we just had to make sure that no one came in and used it while they were splashing around in there. We should never have had that last thought – we were getting frivolous already. We had to agree, however, that there *was* a very real danger if the lid was left up when the chicks were about to fledge. We could picture the scene. They had been flexing their wings for days, getting ready for their first historic flight. Then what happens? They leap out of the nest – flap, flap – then plummet, as all young birds do on their first

RSPB/George McCarthy

One of our Robins looking very pleased at having chosen such an entertaining nest site.

flight. But they don't land safely on the ground. No, they plop straight down the pan and get flushed away. Sad, but undeniably funny. And it got worse. What if people had Robins nesting in a disused toilet which didn't have a proper lid on it? Perhaps they should cover it with cling film. This immediately conjured up visions of baby Robins leaping out and bouncing up and down on it like a trampoline.

The more we discussed it, the sillier and gigglier we got. As the time for the live broadcast loomed closer, we attempted to do a rehearsal. The plan was

that we would be sitting next to each other in The Birdmobile. Bill would say:

'Well, we've had lots of letters asking us all sorts of questions. Here's a very interesting one from a viewer who asks: "Shouldn't we put the seat down on the toilet where the Robins are nesting?" Well, Peter, you're the expert . . . what's the answer to that one?'

At which point, Peter would give a perfectly serious response.

We tried it. Not a chance. It took Bill several

attempts to get the question out. When he did, Peter's only reply was a big grin. We tried again. This time, he got three or four words out before dissolving into giggles. Which of course made Bill laugh. Even the sound in our earpieces was of growing hysteria.

By this time, we were nearly on the air. We came to a rapid agreement. Bill would start outside The Birdmobile, where Peter couldn't see him. Bill would introduce the programme by saying simply:

'Let's go over to Peter, who will answer some of your questions.'

We would then cut to Peter inside The Birdmobile – alone. He would read out the letter about the toilet seat, and answer the question. As long as he was by himself, he reckoned he'd just about get through it. Bill was therefore banned from joining him. Instead, he had to lurk outside, waiting till that bit was over. Then he could enter The Birdmobile and take his place alongside Peter. Even then, however, it was agreed that he would on no account look at him.

So that is what we did. And we got away with it . . . just. Anyone watching, and knowing what was going on, would have maybe noticed just a tiny little suppressed gulp as Peter read out the question. And you would also have been aware of two people trying very hard not to look at each other. Of course, the second the broadcast was over, we all collapsed in hysterics. We'd like to think the Robins joined in too. Maybe that's why they nested there in the first place.

Oh by the way, we did put the lid down before the youngsters fledged and, actually, it was just as well. Sure enough, they fluttered out of the nest and landed straight on the lid. As it happened, this was very shiny and slippy, and most of the fledglings skidded off it, ending up on the floor anyway. Every time they hopped back on and tried to take off, their little feet spun round as if they were on ice and they usually slid off again. Eventually they realized that the windowsill provided a rather firmer footing and, one by one, they negotiated the jagged edge of the hole in the window and escaped into the outside world. The whole process took them a few days longer than if the nest had been outside in the garden. This may well have given them a much better chance of survival as, by the time they did escape, they were bigger and better able to fend for themselves. So perhaps they didn't nest in that toilet just for laughs. It was actually a very wise choice.

LOCKED IN!

It was day one of series one and everything was new. The pictures, when the link-ups were established, were fantastic. In fact it was hard to believe that they were live, it all seemed too good to be true.

That Monday was a long day in the field, punctuated by two short programmes for Children's Television during the day and a half-hour programme at 7.30 pm. Once that 'big one' had gone out there was only a 30-second slot between the *Nine O'clock News* and *The Weather* left to do and Peter was scheduled to do it.

Bill went off to watch Peregrines in the Avon Gorge and Peter was left with not a lot to do for two hours as there was a limit to how much he could rehearse a thirty-second programme, especially as no one could predict whether the birds would be awake or asleep by that time.

After exploring every corner of the rather nice garden, but keeping carefully away from the Blue Tits' nest, it suddenly occurred to him that he had not actually seen the real nest except on the monitor. He asked James, the researcher, if he could look inside the little shed which contained the camera and which had the nest box fixed to the side.

Now it may have looked like a small garden shed, but it had been erected courtesy of the BBC and it contained a large tripod with a camera, the cable for the fibre-optic lights and lots of other wires.

'No problem,' said James, 'it won't disturb the birds, once you're in, I'll drop the catch and you can stay in as long as you like.'

It was great, if a little crowded, in the shed. There was the beautifully lit nest box, looking so much smaller after the images we had been watching. The adults kept coming in and the whole family was quite oblivious to the viewer in the shed. It was like watching a tiny theatre.

But time passed all too quickly, the time for the programme was approaching and Peter got ready to leave. But James had gone off and was preparing for the programme back in the 'communications vehicle'. Peter was locked in and any attempt to shout was likely to scare the birds.

Eventually a passing technician noticed the door rattling and, curious to see why, opened it to find a very worried presenter ready to spring back to his place in The Birdmobile.

But there might have been another end to the story. If the technician had not found Peter the programme could still have gone out, cameras would have rolled; no presenter, never mind for 30 seconds let's look in on the Blue Tits . . . and there would have been Peter jumping up and down and waving in the background. There might have been extra drama if the Blue Tit had tried to feed him!

NEST BOXES GALORE

Much of Britain's most productive wildlife habitat is on Ministry of Defence territory. There are several reasons for this. Perhaps most importantly, much of the land is not farmed or developed but left to grow naturally. Secondly, a lot of the habitat is rather specialized: heathland, meadows, scrub or coastland. Thirdly, it is largely undisturbed. This might seem an odd comment considering that military exercises usually include troops, tanks and explosives, but the truth is that none of that disturbance is anything like as damaging to wildlife and natural vegetation as free public access. Moreover, the MOD has a very knowledgeable and authoritative environmental department, who make sure that the manoeuvres avoid sensitive areas.

There is one such military area on Salisbury Plain. Of course, normally, there is no public access, but we on _Bird in the Nest_ were privileged to get a guided tour by Major Lewis, whose Little Owls played such a prominent part in the second series. The major had organized and carried out a splendidly elaborate nest-box scheme over a very wide area, setting up a network of potential nest sites, using old ammunition boxes, which required little more modification than the provision of an entrance hole, and sometimes a few extra partitions inside. As the major represented the Hawk and Owl Trust, most of the boxes were intended to attract species from those families. Smaller boxes were intended for Little Owls, larger ones for Barn Owls and Kestrels.

We were amazed at how close some of the birds would nest. One site had two boxes on the same tree only a few feet apart. There was a family of Kestrels in one of them and a family of Barn Owls in the other. The only occasional snag is that other species are also attracted to these desirable residences and they don't always stick to the rules. The major could put a notice up saying 'Barn Owls only' but it wouldn't work. He had evidence from one box in which, when he cleared it out, he discovered eggs of

Owls. In fact, Jackdaws tend to take over in other situations too. They have a habit of dropping sticks down any hole they think might lead to a suitable nest site and they don't always know when to stop. Sometimes they choose chimneys and their stick dropping builds up a huge pile in the hearth beneath. This becomes a monster-sized nest (if it doesn't become a roaring fire first). Equally, they will drop sticks down holes in trees, even if they are already occupied. The major told us that he had once found a Tawny Owl sitting on its eggs, with a pile of twigs on top of it.

In truth, though, such incidents merely added to the fascination of the nest-box scheme. Despite avian squatters and intruders, the vast majority of the boxes were being used by the right species. The result is that this part of Salisbury Plain has a truly wonderful population of Owls and Kestrels: far more than there were only a few years ago. What's more, they are protected by Her Majesty's Armed Forces, thanks to Major Lewis.

Mandarin Duck, Kestrel and Tawny Owl, all of which had been finally ousted by a Grey Squirrel. Similarly, Jackdaws often grab the boxes intended for Little

More recycling: a (clean) ex-Army sock is used to make sure that the young Owls don't escape before they've been ringed.

Bill Oddie

A family of young Kestrels in one of Major Lewis's ammunition/nest boxes.

Bill Oddie

Bill Oddie

The ring bears a number and asks any finder to inform the British Museum. All part of the scheme administered by the British Trust for Ornithology.

Bill Oddie

It was a privilege to meet our stars at such close quarters. They remained completely calm at all times, even if we didn't.

Video Diary

The photographs in this chapter are taken directly from the BBC video of *Bird in the Nest* and show the remarkable growth rate of four of our twelve species.

SWALLOWS

(*Opposite page*) We first saw our family of Swallows when they were about a week old. They were no longer pink and helpless as they would have been when they first hatched but their feathers had not broken out of their protective sheaths.

(*Top*) By the fourth day of the series the tips of the feathers began to appear and the red faces began to become obvious.

(*Bottom*) By the last programme the young had not left the nest, but their flight feathers had grown and they were looking like short-tailed versions of their parents as they began to exercise their wings and climb around the nest in preparation for their first flight.

BLUE TITS

(*Opposite page*) In programme one, our young Blue Tits were very small, some had not opened their eyes and there was lots of bare pink skin visible, although the quill cases were starting to show where feathers would soon grow.

(*Top*) By the fourth day of the series, their feathers had grown, their eyes had opened, but the patches of bare skin were still quite large.

(*Bottom*) By our last day they were quite adventurous and at least one had explored the farthest corner of the nest box. Their feathers were almost fully grown, they were looking rather like their parents and we expected they would go any day. In fact, they were to stay for much longer than any of us expected.

PEREGRINES

(*Opposite page*) This photo was taken four days before our first programme, when the young were about 16 days old. At this stage they had lots of white fluffy down, but were making plenty of noise when they were expecting a feed.

(*Top*) By the fourth day of the series their down had almost disappeared and we watched them scratch away the last small white feathers. Only the back of the head and parts of their wings presented a removal problem.

(*Bottom*) By our last day our 'babies' were as large as their parents and lots of their time was spent madly flapping their wings, strengthening their muscles for their first flight. They also spread out along the cliff ledge, so it was quite unusual to find all three together.

WOODPECKERS

(*Opposite page*) This photo was taken when the young were about a week old. They were blind, naked and helpless and looking very reptilian. It was about this time that the male Woodpecker was killed.

(*Top*) By the fourth day of the series they were looking much more like Woodpeckers, their black and white feathers were emerging and they were developing red crowns, the hallmark of the young 'Great Spot'.

(*Bottom*) By our last programme the young Woodpeckers were only a few days from flying. They were climbing up the inside of their hole so as to be first to get the food brought by their mother.

The Struggle to Survive

What is the future for our birds once they're out of the nest? If you saw many programmes of either series you will know that our answer to this question is likely to be *cats*!

But really it's not that simple, birds face other dangers and yet many do seem to defy the odds and survive to become parents themselves. So let's take a quick look into the crystal ball and predict the future for our babies once they became 'Bird out of the Nest'.

PEREGRINES

Let's start with the Peregrines. Three healthy looking young: one male and two females. Their first flight will not have taken them far and they will continue to be looked after by their parents for two months. During that time they must develop the skill of hunting or they will not survive.

For the first few weeks out of the nest the adults continue to provide all the food the young need, but the young are encouraged to chase their parents before the prey is passed over and sometimes it is passed from adult to juvenile in mid-air.

Like most youngsters, they like to play but, being Peregrines, they play in flight. The games will help their development, and they chase and dive at each other or talon-grapple, with one bird briefly upside-down below the other. They will also make mock attacks on passing birds but are unlikely to strike them, at least during the first few weeks.

The young are also naturally curious. They have been seen attacking insects, tussocks of grass and even trying to grasp floating seaweed. There are also reports of adult Peregrines catching live prey and releasing it near the young, presumably as a way of encouraging them to hunt. Gradually the birds become more experienced and two months after their first flight they are hunting for themselves.

As autumn approaches, they start to move away from the nest and from their parents. If they find an unoccupied territory nearby they may stay around it for the winter, if not they will wander to lowland areas, usually near the coast. The next summer they are likely to return to the main breeding areas or the edges of the breeding territories but they are unlikely to stay at any particular site.

Not all our young Peregrines will survive. The first twelve months are the hardest and two out of three probably won't be alive next spring. Those that do make it will be the fittest and most successful. It will be two or more years before they take their places on a breeding eyrie and by then they will have all the skills necessary to catch and kill sufficient prey for their own young.

Peregrines have few enemies apart from humans: lack of food, bad weather and accidents are the worst killers. In Europe Eagle Owls will attack and kill Peregrines, but Eagle Owls are not found in the British Isles. Humans, however, continue to be a threat.

The sport of falconry has been practised for more than 2,000 years. Today Peregrines can be bred in captivity and wild birds are protected but still wild

Peregrines are dramatic birds and seem to pick dramatic sites for their nests.

birds are taken illegally and some are smuggled out of the country.

Birds of prey have a popular following, but they are also loathed by some people who carry out other field sports, and each year some Peregrines are shot around Grouse moors and other shooting estates. Another anti-Peregrine group are people who race Pigeons and again many Peregrine eggs or young are illegally destroyed in popular Pigeon-racing areas.

KESTRELS

Our young Kestrels were late developers but all three young left successfully about 28 days after hatching, but they probably returned to their nest site many times because that is where the parents would continue to take the food.

Rather like their Peregrine cousins they stay around their nest site and expect their parents to carry on feeding them. After a week or so they become more daring and sometimes they will snatch food from their parents' talons in mid-air.

Gradually they learn to hunt for themselves and become independent of their parents. After about a month they will start to move away from their nest site. Once they have left they appear to wander up to about 80 miles until they find an area without other Kestrels and with plenty of food. If the food supply holds out they will stay for the winter, if not they will move on.

With the arrival of autumn, some Kestrels have the urge to migrate. This urge is greatest in continental Kestrels, but in the British Isles those living farthest north are the most likely to move south and young birds will probably go farther than adults. As our youngsters live in south-west England they will probably not move very far.

Many Kestrels die during their first year. Only one in three will survive until the next spring, but once they become adult the chance of survival increases. Starvation is the most common cause of death of young Kestrels, especially in autumn and midwinter. If the population of voles is high, then more young Kestrels will survive. The bad news for our Kestrels

Kestrels are equally at home on a remote sea cliff or on a window ledge in the centre of a busy city.

is that the later broods, like ours, often have the lowest survival rate because by the time they are out of the nest and independent, the best feeding areas have been taken over by older birds.

LITTLE OWLS

Our nest had four young which is a good number. In Britain most nests contain either two or three young; only eight per cent have four, so it was little wonder that we saw both parents working hard and frantically active when food was abundant.

As we saw on our night watches, the young can be adventurous. Some will leave the nest before being able to fly properly and, depending on the site, will perch on nearby branches and take cover if one of the adults gives a warning.

Within a week of leaving the nest they are able to fly, but parents will continue to feed them for a further three weeks. Then they need to develop the skill of hunting; earthworms are not too difficult but small mammals such as mice, voles and shrews are rather more challenging. The survival of our Little Owls will depend on the amount of food available and their own ability to catch it. Unfortunately, it is likely that two or three will not live for more than four months.

The surviving young may stay with their parents until September, then the young will spread out over a few miles and search out a territory of their own. During October and November there is some territorial activity, presumably as old and young birds divide up the best feeding and roosting areas; there is much more activity from January through to April when single birds pair up and suitable territories are established ready for the next breeding season.

Little Owls are likely to keep the same partners until one of them dies but, having survived the first year, the chances of survival improve and some live as long as nine or ten years.

Little Owls always have wonderful expressions on their faces.

KINGFISHERS

Of course our first brood of young Kingfishers did not survive – and how many times must that happen without anyone realizing? But what would have happened to the second brood?

Young Kingfishers leave their nest about 24 days after hatching, but they may delay for a day or two if food is in short supply. For the first two days out of the nest the young perch in trees and bushes a hundred metres or more from the nest hole and call for their parents to feed them. But after a few days the parents become aggressive towards their offspring and drive them away. At this time the young will probably not have learned to fish for themselves.

For several weeks the young can be recognized from their parents by their black feet and white tips

RSPB/Susan Boucny

The Kingfisher is a master fisherman whose rapid dives take its prey by surprise.

to their bills and we know that after being driven from their parents' territory the young must find an unoccupied stretch of river and learn to catch their own food. It is not easy and within two months over half the young will have died, mostly from lack of food or drowning.

Even for the survivors there are hard times ahead. Ice in winter can make fishing impossible and the birds will have to find new ice-free areas. Flooding can also make fishing difficult. By spring only one in four will have survived.

GREAT SPOTTED WOODPECKER

Our four young Woodpeckers seem to be survivors. Having grown up with only a mother to feed them they will face their biggest challenge when they leave the nest. Obviously the busy road is a worry; having claimed the life of their father and it would be all too easy for one or more of the young to die in the same way.

The usual behaviour is for the newly fledged Woodpeckers to stay in the area of the nest for a few days and gradually wander farther away, with the brood split between male and female. It will be a big task for the female to continue to look after all four young on her own.

Young Great Spotted Woodpeckers will start to feed themselves on their first day out of the nest, but they will also beg to be fed. Gradually they become more adept at finding their own food and less dependent on the adult. But they are in danger from predators such as a Sparrowhawk; weaker youngsters may fall victim to a Crow and those nesting in or near gardens may be caught by the dreaded cat.

One of the first problems young Woodpeckers need to solve for themselves is where to roost. For the first two nights out of the nest they may sleep clinging on to trees but soon they will learn to find suitable holes to roost in.

Those that survive will move to local woods or copses, and perhaps visit other gardens, but they are unlikely to travel more than a few miles from their original nest.

RSPB/Roger Wilmshurst

Great Spotted Woodpeckers will visit gardens in winter in search of food, but it is unusual for them to stay to nest.

SWALLOWS

The five Swallows all left their nest successfully. First they moved out on to a nearby beam in the barn roof then, after a few days, they launched themselves into the air for the first time.

They continue to be fed by their parents for a few weeks and may return to their nest at night, but being a first brood they will have to become independent quickly because their parents will want to raise at least one more brood before the summer ends.

During July, the young Swallows leave their farmyard and move to wherever local Swallows are gathering to feed. This is a dangerous time because numbers of inexperienced Swallows are an easy target for birds of prey such as Sparrowhawks and, especially, Hobbies.

Gradually the flock of Swallows becomes larger and at night they roost together in reeds or other tall vegetation. Then, some time in August, they will start their remarkable migrational journey to South Africa. They will travel mainly in small groups and fly in a southerly direction. They fly by day (which is unusual, as many small birds migrate at night) because they do not need to stop and feed and they can catch what food they need as they fly. Their journey may be erratic; fast over land, but slow to take advantage of good feeding over a lake or reservoir. At night, groups will join together at a suitable roost.

Many of their migration routes will take them along river valleys but they will cross high land as well. The sea is a natural barrier and here they may pause until they have a following wind to take them to France and on to Spain. They will tend to avoid the highest land of the Pyrenees, passing through valleys or following the coast.

The next sea crossing is the Mediterranean, and many will follow the coast until they come to the natural crossing at Gibraltar. Others will make longer sea crossings and in bad weather numbers will gather on the Mediterranean islands.

Once in Africa the next natural barrier is the Sahara Desert. Many will avoid it by following the coast, but others will cross, pausing at oases to rest and feed. Onward they go, across the grasslands of the savannas, the tropical forests around the equator, and still on until they reach almost the very southern tip of the African continent. Of all the Swallows migrating from Europe to Africa, those from the British Isles go the farthest, choosing to winter in the balmy summer of the Cape Province in South Africa, a journey of more than 5,000 miles.

This amazing journey will take about eight weeks, so our Swallows will be arriving some time in October. Once there they will find plenty of food and they will start to moult their feathers. Although they will have another summer when they arrive, there is no evidence that they attempt to breed, although the local Swallows will be busy rearing their young.

About January or February they begin their northward journey. The urge to breed and the weather conditions in spring will help them to make the return journey in about six weeks.

The ability of these young birds to navigate back to the same area as they left the year before is one of those amazing feats that we still cannot fully explain.

The journey has its casualties, of course, and as many as four out of every five young Swallows may die within their first year. Adults that have completed the journey have a longer life expectancy and some birds are known to have survived for at least 15 years.

Bill Oddie

Young Swallows will make a 3,000 mile journey to South Africa within a few weeks of leaving the nest.

PIED WAGTAILS

We only know of one young Pied Wagtail which survived from our nest in the tractor but it is very likely that its parents will have nested again and reared another family.

Normally, as soon as one youngster flies from the nest the parents will encourage the others to follow so that the family stays together. They will remain around the nest site for the first day but, by the second day, they will move off. That night will be spent at a roost away from the nest.

The young Wagtails are fed by their parents for between four and seven days. The male finds most of the food for the first brood as, already, the female is preparing for her second family.

Once independent, the young Wagtails move away from the nesting area and sometimes join small flocks of other Wagtails. At night, communal roosts of mainly young Wagtails start to form and as autumn approaches these roosts start to attract migrant Wagtails from other parts of Britain or, in some places, migrants from the continent.

These winter roosts may be surprisingly large and in unusual places. Traditionally they are in reed beds and other vegetation, but sewage farms are also used – the birds sitting on the rotating arms of sewage treatment equipment throughout the night. There are several urban roosts of Pied Wagtails, one famous one was in plain trees in Dublin for more than thirty years. Recently, motorway service stations have been used.

During the winter some adult males will defend what is sometimes called a feeding territory, which is an area alongside a river that has a good food supply and from which it will chase other Pied Wagtails. Some males will, however, tolerate a second bird (called by scientists a 'satellite') if this extra bird helps to defend the territory and doesn't threaten the occupying male. Many of these 'satellites' are juveniles.

Once again the first year is the most dangerous for a Pied Wagtail and three out of four die before they have a chance to rear their own young. But some adults are surprisingly long lived. The oldest bird we know of survived nine years and eleven months.

RSPB./Michael W Richards

Pied Wagtails are not always seen near water and they are quite often seen running about in car parks.

ROBINS

We rather think that our brood of Robins in the loo may have been their second brood. Although it was certainly the first nest in the loo, the same pair may already have had an earlier brood somewhere else, or their first nest had been lost for some reason but we really don't know.

The young did take a little while to find their way out of the broken window and it was unlikely they would return once they were out, although young Robins will sometimes return to their old nest to roost. It is quite normal for young Robins to leave the area of the nest quickly, even though they can only fly weakly for four or five days and a lot of their time is spent on the ground.

Both male and female will normally take part in feeding and looking after their young and they may even divide up the brood between them, but if there is going to be another brood then the female gives up early and leaves the feeding to the male. After about ten days the young are learning to feed themselves and their parents give them rather less food, until they give up all together after perhaps 16 days and usually by 24 days.

Once they can feed themselves the young Robins are fully independent, they wander round their parents' territory for a time and then travel farther away, but usually no more than a mile. There they will moult and get their red breast for the first time and also try to establish their own territory. As the adults start to moult they are less aggressive and the juveniles find life quite easy at first but, as the adult pairs start to separate and set up their winter territories, the young Robins have to fight to hold their ground, and many are evicted. Young female Robins have a tendency to migrate at this time and therefore

may leave the area all together, the others will gradually sort out their territories by October when the winter weather sets in.

Both males and females hold winter territories and defend them fiercely; only early in the new year will a Robin's courtship begin and pairs start to form. Both birds will then defend the territory.

Why do Robins perch on spade handles? The spade provides them with a good perch to spot their prey from.

RSPB/M K Walker

STARLINGS

The future of our four Starlings' eggs is anyone's guess. If we are right in thinking that this was a second brood, then the young should have hatched within 12 days of the eggs being laid, and the young would have left the nest three weeks after that.

As a second brood, their chances of survival would have been less than that of the first brood which will have joined flocks of hundreds, even thousands of other young Starlings which roam the countryside in summer looking for supplies of food and roosting together among bushes or reeds. The second broods are out at a time when food becomes harder to find but, whereas the early brood will have left their parents quickly, these later youngsters stay with their parents for about a month.

As autumn approaches small groups of adults and juvenile Starlings join together and often form large flocks. Sometimes these flocks feed with other birds such as Thrushes, Golden Plovers or Gulls. They will roost with other Starling flocks; at suitable roosts flock after flock will arrive and join in impressive aerobatics before settling down for the night.

Both the summer and winter flocks attract predators. Both Sparrowhawks and, it would appear from our live pictures on *Bird in the Nest*, Peregrines will feed on Starlings. Despite these attacks the survival rate of young Starlings is better than that of other small birds, perhaps that is why they are generally a successful species.

However, we must not be too confident about the future of Starlings, because recent surveys have shown that the number breeding each year is falling and even the big winter flocks appear to be fewer and smaller. The reason is far from clear, but changes in farming methods are a likely cause as much of a Starling's life is spent on some type of farmland.

RSPB/Roger Wilmshurst

We rather take Starlings for granted, but they are really very attractive birds.

JACKDAWS

Our two young Jackdaws will have flown within a few days but are unlikely to move very far. Jackdaws in northern and upland areas of the British Isles may migrate away to downland in the south, or move south west and often join flocks of other Jackdaws and Rooks. Our family in south-west England is likely to remain local and continue to roost in its colony.

Young Jackdaws survive rather well; indeed their chances of surviving their first year are better than all the other species which have appeared in the programmes. There are dangers, of course, and especially as they leave the nest for the first time. At this stage they can barely fly and, if one is less well developed than the other, it may sit helplessly under its nest and, for a time, will be very vulnerable to any predators.

The parents remain with the young throughout the first day and night and soon the young will move away to join a group of other young Jackdaws, although they will continue to be fed by their parents. While the Jackdaw flock is unlikely to go far it will range over the locality in search of the best feeding places. Adults remain in pairs during the winter and may revisit their old nest. Very few young Jackdaws breed in their first spring and it is only by their second year that they will build a nest of their own.

Jackdaws are quite long-lived birds and there is at least one report of one surviving until its 14th year.

Jackdaws are named after their ringing 'jac, jac' calls.

RSPB /Peter Perfect

BLUE AND GREAT TITS

These two closely related species have many characteristics in common, so let's consider the future of both these families at the same time; indeed it is possible that they will come into contact with each other as they struggle to survive their first year as birds out of the nest.

The youngsters usually leave their nest early in the morning, which allows them to get used to their surroundings before dark, because they will not return to their nest. If the last young to leave is very slow it will be encouraged by its parents which want to keep the whole brood together. Adult Great Tits have been seen to try to pull a reluctant youngster from its nest hole.

Although fully feathered when they leave, the flight feathers of the young are not fully grown and they are unable to fly properly for several days and so they do not move far from the nest site. As their flight becomes stronger they move farther from the nest and soon leave the territory altogether.

RSPB/Mark Hamblin

Blue Tits are very popular visitors to gardens and can be attracted close to our windows.

At first the adults bring food to their young, but increasingly the young follow the adults and beg to be fed. Gradually they learn to find their own food and after a few weeks the family party starts to break up. The adults will stop looking after their young sooner if they start a second brood, but in Britain second broods, even for Great Tits, are rare.

Once the young are independent they may move farther away and join wandering flocks of other juvenile Tits but their wanderings are unlikely to take them more than ten miles from their original nest. Some adults may join these flocks while other adults stay around their territories. Some young stay with their parents into the autumn.

Both adults and young will go through a period of moult. The adults will moult all their feathers in about three months, the juveniles will moult their body and tail feathers but keep their flight feathers which have only just reached full size. Once the moult has been completed some adults will start to set up territories, but the onset of winter weather is likely to encourage them to join the wandering flocks, which may include other small birds such as Goldcrests.

There is high mortality among the juveniles during these first months out of the nest. The most common cause of death is starvation, especially of the smaller young, but there are other dangers. In the woods, Jays are on the lookout for inexperienced small birds and will often try to knock them to the ground where they will be easier to catch. But the main predator is the Sparrowhawk which times its own breeding to coincide with the maximum number of fledglings in the woods when its own young need the most food.

Other dangers come from cats, cars and from flying into windows. Young inexperienced birds are most likely to fall to these dangers. Older birds have, presumably, mostly learnt to avoid them, although accidents do still happen.

Winter weather can also be a problem, periods of snow and ice make food hard to find and the death rate rises, especially among the young birds. Survival can also be influenced by the crop of seeds from the beech tree, called 'mast'. In years when this is plenti-ful, and there are sometimes enormous crops, the survival of Great Tits is noticeably better.

A year on, and only a few, perhaps one in five, of our youngsters will have survived but as adults a few will grow to a ripe old age: there are reports of a Blue Tit surviving for 12 years and a Great Tit living to be 15 years old.

Great Tits have a wide range of calls that can cause confusion at first.

RSPB/M K Walker

Your Questions Answered

One of the most interesting spin-offs from *Bird in the Nest* was the number of questions which it generated. There were so many after the first series that the BBC decided to feature more questions in the second series and to have a special telephone line to capture the calls.

So, here we will attempt to answer some of the most common and the most interesting questions.

WHAT DO I DO IF I FIND A BABY BIRD

The simple answer is to leave it alone and let the parents do the job because they are much better at that than we are.

Many young birds, such as Robins, are unable to fly properly for a few days after leaving their nests. They also have little understanding of danger. So people often come across a fledgling in the open and assume it has been abandoned. Often the parents are not far away and will come back once the human disappears. If there are several young birds in the brood, there may be quite long gaps between feeds, which reinforces the impression that the young bird is lost.

Of course there are disasters. Young birds freshly out of the nest will land in dangerous places such as

near roads. Then the advice is to move them to a safe place and leave them alone. If you know where the nest was or where the parents are feeding, then that is the right place, if you don't know and have to guess, then usually placing the bird in thick cover is best. The parents can locate it by its calls.

You should only consider looking after the young birds yourself if you are certain that they are unable to survive in the wild (eg, both adults having been killed) and you should realize that you will be taking on a long, messy and time-consuming job.

Young birds often eat their own weight of food in a day and Robin-sized birds and smaller need feeding at about twenty-minute intervals from dawn to dusk. Most birds will take crushed, soaked digestive biscuit mixed with the yolk of hard-boiled egg and thin strips of raw ox heart (occasionally dusted with SA37 or another vitamin supplement). Also try natural food such as earthworms (large ones should be cut up), small insects, green caterpillars or cut-up mealworms or waxworms (which should be freshly killed before feeding).

Food needs to be pushed well down young birds' throats and blunt forceps should be used if available. You may need to force feed a bird initially but it will soon learn to gape. Generally they should be handled as little as possible and not made into a pet.

The law requires that it is released back into the wild as soon as it is able to fend for itself, so spend time teaching it to pick up its own food and finding the right natural food. Every effort should be made to release it as soon as possible. If you need further advice on looking after individual birds you should contact your local vet or the RSPCA.

SHOULD I CLEAN OUT A NEST BOX AFTER IT HAS BEEN USED?

You should clean out a nest box after it has been used, or even if a nest has been built and then abandoned. The best time to do this is after the nesting season.

The reason is that many parasites live in birds' nests and some of these lie dormant during the winter but emerge the following spring to infest the next

RSPB/S C Porter

The smaller species worked very hard to keep the nest clean and the young birds' droppings were generally carried away from the nest.

family. In the wild, holes tend not to be used every year or are used by a different species of bird or even mammals.

Nest boxes should, however, be left in place all year. Sometimes small birds will use them to roost in, especially in autumn and winter; and if they prove to be suitable roosts then it is possible that they will be selected as nest sites the following year.

HOW DO I GET BIRDS TO USE MY NEST BOX?

The ideal positions are outlined on pages 135–7 but there is no magic solution. Here are some hints of things not to do.

Don't have a nest box with a perch, it is unnecessary

RSPB/Michael Edwards

Garden ponds can be home to a wide variety of wildlife as well as allowing birds to drink and bathe.

and makes it easier for other larger species to look inside and birds like privacy when nesting. Also, don't hang food round the box or put the box too close to a birdtable. The resident birds need their own territory from which they will chase other birds, putting food close to the nest will attract others and your birds will waste energy chasing them off.

One other point to remember, in some years, especially during a spell of mild winter weather, small birds such as Blue Tits may start setting up territories and selecting nest sites as early as January, so get your box up before Christmas.

HOW DO BABY BIRDS GET WATER?

This was an interesting question from a young viewer. Perhaps it is at first surprising that young birds don't need to drink until you think carefully about their food. During spring and summer they are fed mainly on caterpillars and other insects which are themselves full of liquid.

The birds which need to drink most often are those that feed on seeds, nuts and other dry foods, however, even finches which specialize in these foods feed their young on insects.

Pigeons are different; although they eat grain and plant material, they partly digest their food which is stored in a form of milk for their young. The baby, or 'squab', puts its beak down its parent's throat to obtain its food.

But irrespective of what most birds eat they do need access to water throughout the year in order to bathe, because bathing helps keep their feathers in good trim.

SHOULD I FEED THE BIRDS IN MY GARDEN IN SUMMER?

With caution, summer feeding can be helpful to garden birds but remember to provide water as well (see pages 132–3).

HOW DO I STOP CATS CATCHING BIRDS IN MY GARDEN?

One of the most distressing occasions for anyone who cares for their garden birds is to find a local cat with one of 'their' birds in its paws. Cats are unnatural predators in gardens and are responsible for millions of birds' deaths each year. Cats hunting birds has little to do with whether the cat is hungry or not, it is a way for the cat to keep its hunting skills in trim.

There are a number of deterrents worth considering for your garden. If the cat is your own, then you should consider putting a bell round its neck to act as an early warning to the bird population. Also, cats can be trained to avoid a garden by the reception they receive: once soaked by the spray from a hose they are unlikely to return. There are also high-frequency alarms which emit a signal that deters cats, but is inaudible to other animals.

One view which will comfort those who own a cat is that it just may be better to keep it than get rid of it, for the reason that its territory, which is your garden, is less likely to be visited by other cats. Remove your cat and you might have several others move in.

Cats catch and kill millions of birds each year.

CAN I PREVENT MY RACING PIGEONS FROM BEING ATTACKED BY PEREGRINES?

Peregrines are also known as Pigeon-hawks because they will catch Pigeons if they are available. Most Pigeons were once wild Rock Doves, but now Rock Doves are rather rare and Peregrines turn their attention to other medium-sized birds, which includes Racing Pigeons if they happen to pass through the Peregrines' feeding area.

Whether the Peregrines take the fastest or slowest Pigeons is questionable. There is evidence from some eyries that the majority of Pigeons we caught have already lost their way.

But what can the Pigeon-racer do? Well, a recent invention may help. Owl-eye patterns can now be transferred on to the Pigeon's wings. These two large artificial eyes do not affect the bird's flight, but they deter the Peregrine before it strikes. This method of scaring your enemy is not uncommon in nature; butterflies and moths have evolved this method of survival over millions of years.

HOW LONG DO BIRDS LIVE?

There is no easy answer to this because it differs for each species. We know about some species which have been kept in captivity but as those are unusual circumstances, they are probably not typical. The only reliable records are of those birds which have been ringed when young and live wild. Only a small proportion are ever recovered and many of those recoveries are of young or inexperienced birds which died in an unnatural way.

From the records we have we know that the average life expectancy is surprisingly short. A Robin, for example, has an average lifespan of 13 months. We also hear occasionally about individuals which are surprisingly old; over 12 years for one Robin. So how do we reconcile these two facts?

The main threats for most species come in the first few months out of the nest, with a generally very high mortality before the first anniversary of hatching. Once birds have seen the year round the chances for survival get a little better.

This is the maximum age recorded so far for each of our birds:

Peregrine	15 years 6 months
Kestrel	16 years 2 months
Little Owl	15 years 7 months
Great Spotted Woodpecker	10 years 9 months
Kingfisher	15 years 5 months
Swallow	15 years 11 months
Pied Wagtail	9 years 11 months
Robin	12 years 9 months
Blue Tit	12 years 4 months
Great Tit	15 years
Jackdaw	14 years 3 months
Starling	20 years 1 month

WHEN ARE BIRDS OLD ENOUGH TO NEST

Most birds are able to breed at a year old. But some, especially the larger species such as the Mute Swan, do not breed until at least their second year and often it is their third or fourth year.

Others, like our Jackdaws, may be capable of breeding at one year old, but often do not find a suitable mate or a suitable site and so delay until the following year.

HOW CAN I STOP MAGPIES TAKING THE EGGS AND YOUNG OF MY GARDEN BIRDS?

Magpies have arrived in many urban and suburban areas within the last twenty years and generally their arrival has not been welcomed, because during the spring and early summer a substantial proportion of the Magpie's diet is eggs and the young of smaller species. This fact, linked with the recent decline in small-bird populations, has led to a call for the number of Mapies to be controlled.

Research has shown that small-bird populations have declined just as much in areas without Magpies and that the cause is more likely to be linked to changes in agricultural practices than to the increase in the Magpies' population. No one is denying that Magpies eat the young of other species but there are some ways you can help to protect garden birds.

Try to make it more difficult for the Magpie to find the nests by planting plenty of shrubs and bushes. Leave corners with tangled vegetation. Leave shed or garage doors open: Robins and Blackbirds may nest inside, but Magpies will probably keep away. If you do have a vulnerable site, then protect it with wire once the eggs have hatched (if you interfere too much at the egg stage, the birds may desert).

HOW CAN I PREVENT SQUIRRELS TAKING THE FOOD I PUT OUT FOR BIRDS?

Attracting birds to your garden may also attract other animals, especially squirrels. Grey squirrels are popular with some people, but hated by others. They can be very determined and, once they have learned to reach your bird food, they are likely to return again and again.

Bill Oddie

Grey Squirrels were introduced from North America and can be a real pest for the wildlife gardener.

They are usually very difficult to deter because they are so agile. Their sharp teeth can chew their way into wooden or plastic feeders and only heavy-duty metal ones are likely to defeat them.

There is, however, some advice for bird-gardeners which may beat most squirrels. A birdtable, erected on a smooth metal post, or with a wide 'collar' near the top and placed away from trees and bushes, is one ploy. Another is to suspend a nut feeder from a thin, horizontal wire and, if the squirrels learn to tightrope walk, then thread two plastic lemonade bottles through to rotate at either end.

Perhaps the simplest way is to buy a commercially produced, squirrel-proof feeder which is really a normal feeder suspended inside a small cage that allows small birds in and out, but excludes larger species, including squirrels.

WHERE DO BIRDS GO TO DIE?

This may seem a rather macabre question until you think about it.

During the programmes we emphasized that most of the young birds we watched would probably die before they became adults. Considering the millions of young birds of all species which hatch each spring it is, perhaps, surprising that we are not knee-deep in dead fledglings.

Those we do see tend to be those which came to an unnatural end, such as flying into a window, hitting a car or being caught by a cat. The rest tend to die where we don't see them, perhaps caught by a predator, such as a weasel or a Sparrowhawk, or they die at night in their roosts.

The bodies of birds soon disappear, as they are a source of food for other birds such as Crows and mammals such as Hedgehogs, Badgers and Foxes.

Those that are missed soon decompose with the help of flies and worms. In fact this is the ultimate recycling and nothing is wasted, all returns to the environment.

WHERE DO BIRDS SLEEP

Considering how much we now know about birds, this is a subject that has not been well studied.

Where birds sleep depends on the species. All species disappear for part of the day, whether it is during the hours of darkness for most species, or the hours of daylight for species such as Owls and Nightjars. For many waders and wildfowl, they may be active at night if the tide is out and food is available.

Some species, such as Robins and Woodpeckers, will roost alone; Starlings and others will roost in huge flocks and some like Long-tailed Tits roost huddled with others for warmth.

A good roost needs to be safe from predators and protected from the worst weather. Ducks, Geese and Swans roost on water and many larger ground-nesting birds, such as Pheasants, will roost in trees and bushes. Many others roost as individuals sheltering in dense bushes. Treecreepers cram themselves into a crevice or make their own in the soft bark of the Wellingtonia tree.

Nearly all Swallow nests are built in man-made structures such as barns and sheds.

RSPB

There are some fascinating exceptions: some birds roost in flight. Swifts have been shown by radar to fly to a thousand metres or more and spend the night on the wing. First year non-breeding birds do this, and adults often join them later in the summer. In their winter quarters in Africa, it is very likely that this is their normal method of roosting.

WHY DO SOME BIRDS HOP AND OTHERS WALK?

This is one of those questions that seems to bother quite a lot of people, but it doesn't seem to bother the birds much!

The species which hop, such as most small song birds and Crows, are those which live in trees. Those which run or walk, such as waders and Wagtails, are birds which habitually find their food on the ground.

How You Can Help

Over eight million people watched *Bird in the Nest*; if they all did something to help wild birds then together we really could make a big difference. We know that the populations of many birds are falling and humans are changing the environment in many ways; it is all too easy to say that someone should do something, but often the answer is that it is *we* who should do something and this chapter gives a few practical ideas.

IN THE GARDEN

Most people have a garden and these gardens are rather important habitats for many species of birds, and indeed other animals as well. If you plan for birds and wildlife in your garden you can guarantee hours of pleasure and have the satisfaction of knowing that you are doing something to help.

FEED THE BIRDS

Many people already feed the birds in their gardens. If you use leftover scraps it costs nothing and is a good way of recycling waste food.

Nearly all the food we eat is also suitable for birds, especially in winter when there is no chance of them feeding it to their young. Provided you avoid salted peanuts and desiccated coconut, and chop any bacon rinds, all other unwanted food could be put out in the garden.

You don't really have to have a special container. The scraps can be put on to a lawn, away from any bushes early in the morning: placing it away from bushes is so that cats can't lurk nearby. Early morning

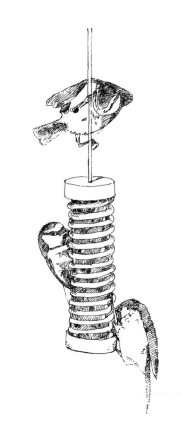

is best so that it has all gone by evening and will not attract mice or rats. However, once you start, it is important to continue, because birds can come to rely on garden-feeding stations and will return daily.

While some of the common species such as House Sparrows and Starlings will eat most of our food, you may want to attract other species as well. To do this you will need to buy some special, fairly inexpensive food for them.

Start with peanuts. These are sold in many places specially for birds (but not salted peanuts because the salt isn't good for them). To be sure that the nuts don't contain bacteria harmful to birds, always use nuts with the 'Safe Nuts' logo.

It is best to put peanuts into some sort of container so small birds like Blue and Great Tits have a chance to get their share. As we have seen these birds are used to feeding by hanging on to food, so the peanut container can be hung from trees and bushes and the Tits will cling on to get their food; other species will find feeding in this way much more difficult, but given time House Sparrows will probably try to copy the Tits.

There is other food you can buy. Wild-bird food is sold by many petshops and is of variable quality. Some is very good and quite cheap, but others contain some quite unsuitable food. Specialist magazines such as the RSPB's *Birds* magazine and *Birdwatching* contain advertisements for mail-order birdfood from specialist suppliers.

Feeding birds through the summer has been debated for many years. Current thinking is that cautious summer feeding is all right but the kitchen scraps of winter should be avoided as the digestive systems of young birds are more delicate than those of their parents and, therefore, unnatural food should be avoided.

The best food of all is, of course, natural food collected by the parents. But gardens are not natural woodlands and natural food can run short. Providing sensible food can help to increase the breeding success of small birds. Specialist wild-bird food should be purchased, especially black sunflower seeds. Large pieces of peanut can kill nestlings, but small pieces can keep them alive, so use a metal feeder with small holes so the birds cannot take too much.

BUILD A BIRDTABLE

Once the birds are used to coming to your garden then you should think of buying a birdtable, or better still, build one yourself. Instructions for a simple design are given on page 132.

The advantage of a birdtable is that the food is off the ground so it will not attract mice and rats, also the high-level feeding will make a successful attack by a cat less likely. A birdtable is also a useful base from which to suspend peanuts and other hanging food for Tits and Greenfinches. It can also be positioned to give the best view from your windows.

One point to remember, however, is that not all birds like to use birdtables; some, such as Song Thrushes and Dunnocks, prefer to feed on the ground, so continue to put small amounts of food on your lawn for those specialist feeders.

PUT OUT WATER

Birds also need water for drinking and for bathing. Bathing is particularly important as it helps to keep their feathers in tip-top condition.

An ornate bird bath is unnecessary as a simple container will do, provided it is not left to dry out. In winter, water is just as important but it must be kept ice-free during spells of severe weather.

BUILD A POND

A good method of introducing water into a garden is by building a pond, which will not only help birds, but it will help other wildlife as well.

A good wildlife pond needs to be a reasonable size, say 1 metre by 2 metres at least and have shallow, sloping edges from which birds can drink and bathe. Introduce some native plants, don't bother with gold-fish, and you will soon have a natural focus of activity in summer and winter. The reason for not

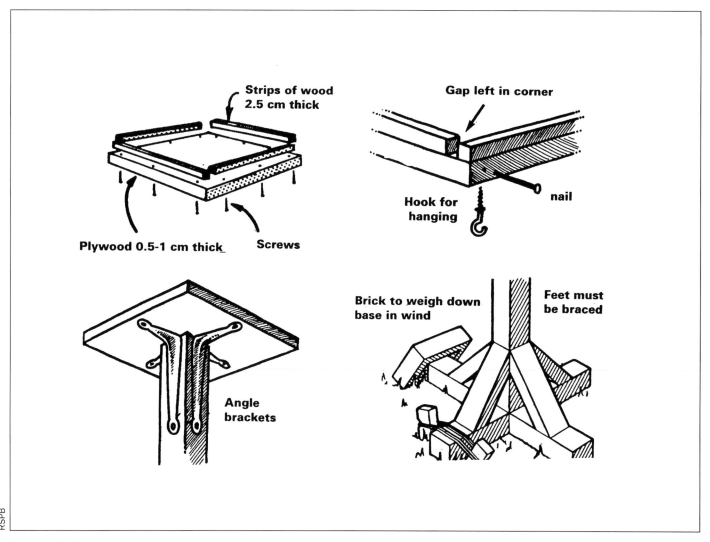

Strips of wood 2.5 cm thick

Plywood 0.5-1 cm thick

Screws

Gap left in corner

Hook for hanging

nail

Angle brackets

Brick to weigh down base in wind

Feet must be braced

Simple design for a bird table

introducing fish is that garden ponds are important breeding ground for frogs, but goldfish will eat the tiny tadpoles.

Ponds help other birds as well. Muddy edges in spring can provide local House Martins with their building material. Blackbirds and Song Thrushes also incorporate mud into their nests and, again, the pond can supply their needs.

BUILD A NEST BOX

Many gardens may have a reasonable amount of food for birds but have a shortage of nest sites. The next addition should, therefore, be a nest box – or even two or three nest boxes. There are two basic designs for the average garden: the one with the

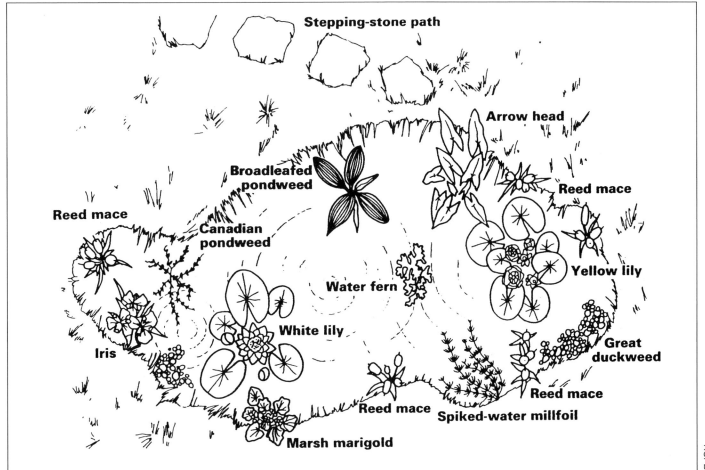

A wildlife pond

RSPB

small hole for Blue Tits and Great Tits and one with an open front, for species such as Robins and, if you are really lucky, Spotted Flycatchers.

Positioning the boxes can be critical. As far as is possible they should not be in a position where enemies such as cats can reach them. The entrances should not face the midday sun, unless heavily shaded, otherwise the boxes will overheat, neither should they face into the prevailing wind or the rain will get in. A position facing north or east is likely to be most successful.

The height of the Tit box should be between 2 and 4 metres, while the open-fronted box could be very low to attract Robins or, again between 2 and 4 metres to attract Spotted Flycatchers. The open-fronted box could be positioned amongst climbing plants, such as ivy or roses.

Having said all that, and made it sound like a science, there does seem to be a lot of luck involved. We both know people who have most unsuitable boxes used regularly and others who have tried hard with different designs in different places, and still failed. What is most likely to affect success is the number of natural nest sites in the area and the number of territories covering the garden. To increase the number of territories you will need to plan your winter and summer feeding carefully and also the plants you introduce.

PLANTING FOR BIRDS

If you view your garden, however small or large, as your own personal nature reserve you can start to plan it from the point of view of wildlife. That does not mean it need be very untidy or that there need be lots of nettles and other 'weeds'. It simply means that the needs of birds are considered as part of the planning.

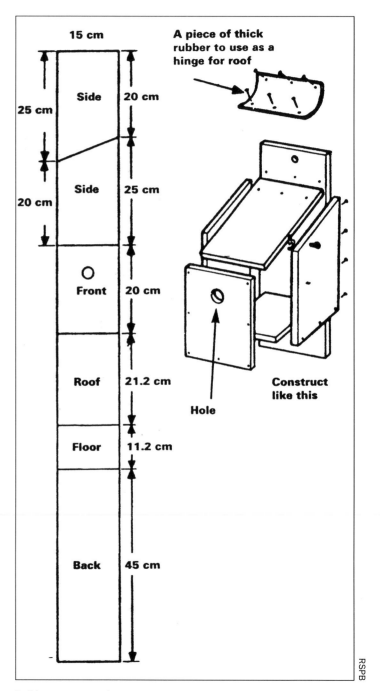

Build your own nest box

Does your garden contain enough cover for birds to hide their nests and are there trees or shrubs which produce berries for birds such as rowan or blackberry? Have you included some native plants such as hawthorn and ivy alongside traditional garden plants? Is there part of the garden that is less disturbed and where birds can feed and even nest in peace. Can you introduce suitable trees such as silver birch and bushes, like hazel or holly, which provide food and shelter?

These simple compromises can help produce a garden which is attractive to both birds and humans. It can be further improved with its buddleia and wild-flower 'meadow' for butterflies, its pond for frogs and newts, its pile of dead wood for invertebrates, its leaf-pile for hedgehogs and its active compost heap.

may rest or even breed in them, and hedgehogs will also explore them in their search for food.

COMPOST

There was a time that every garden had its compost corner. Now with the coming of tidy tips and wheelie bins, many more gardeners dispose of their garden waste elsewhere, which is a pity because a good compost pile is also good for birds and other wildlife.

The whole point of composting is to build up layers of organic material which generates its own heat and contains enough decomposers, from worms to bacteria, to turn the material back into a rich humus as quickly as possible.

Turning over the compost during dry weather in summer, or forking it on to the garden, is a very practical way of helping birds, like Blackbirds and Thrushes, at a time of year when other food may be becoming more difficult to find.

Composts can also be good for other creatures: in rural areas, grass snakes, which are quite harmless,

NEST BOXES FOR OTHER BIRDS

So far we have looked at the most obvious things you can do in your garden, but there are ways of helping some of the other species in *Bird in the Nest* which do not commonly visit gardens.

Kestrels, for example, are found in both town and countryside and will often use a suitable nest box. An example of a successful design is shown on page 136.

Readers with very large gardens might try erecting a box of this kind, but perhaps a discussion with a local farmer or landowner might produce a more appropriate site. Some schools might consider putting a box like this in an inaccessible place, or what about a local churchyard or cemetery? One RSPB Members' Group gained permission to put up Kestrel boxes alongside a motorway.

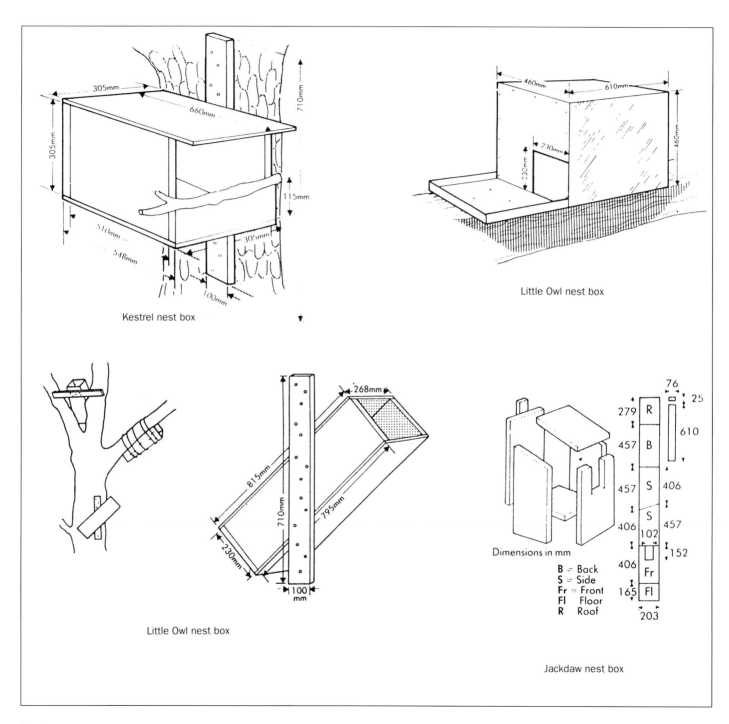

Kestrel nest box

Little Owl nest box

Little Owl nest box

Dimensions in mm

B = Back
S = Side
Fr = Front
Fl = Floor
R = Roof

Jackdaw nest box

Little Owls will, as we saw on the programme, adopt a well-made, artificial nest site, especially in an area where there is a shortage of natural sites. See page 136 for two examples of successful Little Owl box designs.

Jackdaws will adopt a wide variety of natural and unnatural sites. Those in the programmes nested in old, clean oil drums and we heard that the Little Owl boxes were also often taken over by Jackdaws. Another possible design for a Jackdaw box is shown on page 136.

Swallows do not really need much help as they build their own nests of mud but in some areas there may be a shortage of suitable nest sites. If you have Swallows in your locality, and you have a suitable outhouse, garage or shed, perhaps you should consider leaving the door or window open in the spring, or remove a small pane of glass so Swallows can get in and out. A small shelf or even a couple of large nails in a dark corner might help the birds start their nest-building.

In Britain Starlings regularly nest under the eaves of houses, and are often rather unpopular. In other countries they are welcomed and special nest boxes are put up for them. In Russia, it is not unusual for a garden to have several Starling nest boxes – which could be a smaller version of a Jackdaw box – and others to be incorporated into the design of the house; presumably Starlings are popular because of the number of garden 'pests' they eat.

The Pied Wagtail will sometimes use an open-fronted nest box. It is unusual for it to nest in most gardens but there may be other local sites which are more suitable. Again, an inaccessible area of some school or office grounds may provide a very suitable site.

Our story of the Woodpeckers has a few lessons for the gardener. Great Spotted Woodpeckers were attracted to the garden by careful winter feeding. Also an old tree trunk was left in place, long after it was dead. Now dead wood is a good thing to leave anyway, but this particular trunk, which had clematis climbing up it, proved to be the ideal site for the Woodpeckers.

The other species are much more difficult to help. Peregrines have to find their own cliff and Kingfishers dig their own nesting tunnel. However, some landowners have been able to help Kingfishers by building artificial banks close to running water. On one RSPB reserve an artificial tunnel has also been used very successfully.

SUPPORT CONSERVATION ORGANIZATIONS

While there is much that individuals can do to help birds and other wildlife, there is also a need for the concerted action of organizations which can campaign for environmental improvements at a national or even an international level.

Conservation organizations need members in order to be effective. Members provide the funds which get work done and members volunteer to carry out some of the conservation work themselves. Also the numbers of members supporting conservation organizations sends out its own message. For instance, the RSPB, with nearly 900,000 members, is listened to by both government and the media, its size really does make a difference.

Names and addresses of various conservation organizations which you can join are given on page 145.

GET TO KNOW YOUR LOCAL BIRDS

The time will come when you will want to move on from the garden birds. By joining a local or national organization you will find out about local and national nature reserves, and many are good places to visit in order to learn bird identification and also to watch bird behaviour. Some reserves even use close-circuit television to bring you live pictures, just like *Bird in the Nest*.

The real pleasure, however, comes not from the mega-reserves, but from working your own patch, getting familiar with local birds, seeing the effects of changing seasons, watching for yourself the effects of migration and recording the changes in common bird populations from year to year.

Too few bird-watchers really get familiar with their local birds, yet there are hours of pleasure to be gained and, more important, local records help provide important base-line data on which conservation decisions can be made. How often, when a planning proposal threatens a local site, do people say, 'What about the birds, what about the wildlife?' yet there is a lack of evidence to back its claim of being special in any way.

Keeping records is part of the bird-watcher's hobby but sending reports in to a local bird club or county bird recorder is even more important. Taking part in some of the surveys and censuses run by the British Trust for Ornithology is another way of ensuring your local patch is properly recorded for the future.

TAKE ACTION LOCALLY

Local nature conservation depends on local people taking action. Not standing in front of bulldozers but asking questions of parish and local councils, finding out what their policies are, what developments are being planned. There is much that can be done by a local community, there are grants for tree planting,

RSPB/Andrew Hay

Birdwatching is growing in popularity for young and adults alike.

powers for creating local nature reserves, recreation areas can be landscaped to accommodate both people and wildlife.

School grounds can often be improved by incorporating wildlife gardens or conservation areas. This is good for the local environment, but it can also be good education for the pupils if the changes are introduced as part of the curriculum.

Churchyards often have great potential for wildlife. Careful planting and even nest-box schemes can increase the bird populations of these areas.

Discussions with farmers and local landowners can help to raise the profile of birds and conservation (but is not an excuse to trespass); often they don't know what wildlife lives on their land or, if they do, they are glad that someone else appreciates it as well. Being sympathetic may be the first step towards looking after the land better in future.

There are so many ways for local people to build public support for birds and wildlife. If you are a member of a local organization which has visiting speakers, why not invite a local nature reserve warden, county ecologist or someone who can talk about local wildlife? Such sessions invariably end with a fascinating discussion with the audience who contribute their own local stories and observations.

TACKLE THE DECISION MAKERS

If you do see changes taking place locally you will want to make your voice heard. Many decisions are made locally, but a great many more are made by county councils or by central government. But even at this level the local voice is important. Politicians, both local and national, want to please their electorate and, therefore, you need to tell them what you

think about your local environmental issues.

Protests don't have to be on placards outside parliament or in long petitions, a well reasoned letter sent to the right decision maker can be just as effective. It is important that environmentalists are not seen to be negative – positive contributions to a debate are always welcome; the important thing is to get the environment higher on everyone's agenda, because that will be good for the birds and it will also be good for all of us.

ADOPT A GREEN LIFESTYLE

We seem to have come a long way from *Bird in the Nest* but, as we have seen, the populations of many of our birds are very vulnerable to changes in the environment. What we are now learning is that often it is *our* lifestyle that affects the environment.

Saving energy in our homes can also save birds, indirectly. Generating electricity releases sulphur and nitrogen oxides, which creates acid rain, which has been linked to the loss of invertebrates in Welsh streams, which reduces the number of Dippers . . . and, perhaps, Kingfishers?

Depletion of natural resources, air and water pollution, climate change and sea-level rise are current or potential threats to birds, wildlife and to ourselves. Adopting a greener lifestyle does make sense.

This is not the place to detail all the actions we can take, but recycling, cutting down car travel and using public transport, saving energy and water in the home, and buying organically grown food can all help to improve the quality of our life and the quality of the environment. With over eight million viewers we really could make a big difference.

Glossary

Bolus	A ball made up of many insects which is fed to nestlings by Swallows and some other birds.
Brood, a	Young birds in, or just out of, a nest and all from the same clutch.
Brood, to	To sit on young birds (sometimes referring to eggs) to help keep them warm and dry (see incubation).
Clutch	Eggs in nest, all laid by the same female.
Colony	A community of birds.
Courtship	Behaviour aimed at attracting or keeping a mate.
Courtship feeding	Male feeding female as part of courtship, but also valuable in supplying female with extra food.
Eyrie	The nest of a bird of prey.
Fledging	The growing of feathers by a young bird in the nest.
Fledgling	A young bird which has just grown its first set of feathers.
Incubation	The act of sitting on eggs so that the body heat of the adult can be transferred to them.
Juvenile	A young bird out of the nest, but retaining some of its first plumage.
Migration	The seasonal movement of birds (and some other animals) from one place to another, followed by a return movement at another season.

Moult   The natural shedding of feathers. All species change their feathers at least once a year.

Plumage   The name given to the feathers which cover a bird.

Roost   The place where a bird will sleep.

Species   A type of animal or plant which can reproduce itself and produce fertile young.

Stoop   The name given to the rapid flight of a Peregrine as it attacks its prey. It has been estimated the birds may reach speeds of more than 200 mph while stooping.

Territory   The area defended by a bird or a pair of birds, often, but not always, around a nest site.

Bibliography

There is a huge selection of bird books and beginners, not surprisingly, find the choice bewildering. Below we have named just a few and arranged them by subject. We have included a few (marked o/p) which are out of print, but available from local libraries, because we believe that these are still useful books on the subject.

IDENTIFICATION

RSPB Book of British Birds, Peter Holden and J T R Sharrock, Macmillan 1994.
Birdwatcher's Pocket Guide, Peter Hayman, Mitchell Beazley 1988.
The Shell Guide to the Birds of Britain and Ireland, James Ferguson-Lees, Ian Willis and J T R Sharrock, Michael Joseph 1983.

REFERENCE

The AA/RSPB Complete Book of British Birds, Michael Cady and Rob Hume (eds), AA 1992.

GARDEN BIRDS

Birdfeeder Handbook, Robert Burton, Dorling Kindersley 1990.

THE SPECIES

Most of our star birds have had books written about them and these monographs contain lots of fascinating material written by some of Britain's best ornithologists.

Kestrel

The Kestrel, Andrew Village, T & A D Poyser 1990.
The Kestrel, Michael Shrubb, Hamlyn Species Guide 1993.
The Kestrel, G Riddle, Shire Natural History 1990.

Peregrine

The Peregrine Falcon, Derek Ratcliffe, T & A D Poyser 1993.
Peregrine Falcons, Roy Dennis, Colin Baxter 1991.

Little Owl

Owls of Europe, Heimo Mikkola, T & A D Poyser 1983.
Owls, Chris Mead, Whittet 1987.
Owls: Their Natural and Unnatural History, John Sparks and Tony Soper, David and Charles 1989.

Kingfisher

The Kingfisher, David Boag, Shire Natural History 1986.
The Kingfisher, David Boag, Blandford Press 1982 (o/p).
Kingfisher, P Fioratti, HarperCollins 1992.

Swallow

The Swallow, Peter Tate, Shire Natural History 1986.
Swallows, Peter Tate, Witherby 1981 (o/p).
The Swallows, Angela Turner, Hamlyn Species Guide 1994.

Pied Wagtail

British larks, pipits and wagtails, Eric Simms, HarperCollins 1992.

Robin

The Life of the Robin, David Lack, Witherby 1965 (o/p) and Fontana 1970 (o/p).
Robins, Chris Mead, Whittet Books 1984.

Blue and Great Tit

British Tits, Christopher Perrins, Collins 1979 (o/p).
The Great Tit, Andrew Gosler, Hamlyn Species Guide 1993.
The Blue Tit, Jim Flegg, Shire Natural History 1987.

Starling

The Starling, Christopher Feare, Shire Natural History 1985.
The Starling, Christopher Feare, Oxford University Press 1984.

Jackdaw

Crows: a Study of the Corvids of Europe, C J F Coombs, Batsford 1978 (o/p).

Useful Organizations

Watching birds on television or in the garden can be great fun, finding them for yourself in the country-side can be challenging, but to ensure their long-term survival you should join one or more of the national organizations which work to conserve wild birds and the natural environment for the future.

THE ROYAL SOCIETY FOR THE PROTECTION OF BIRDS

The RSPB is Europe's largest voluntary wildlife conservation organization; it works to conserve wild birds and the environment. It has 750,000 adult members and 140,000 young people enrolled in the YOC, its junior section.

The RSPB owns or manages more than 100 nature reserves, to most of which members have free access. It campaigns for a healthy world rich in birds and other wildlife and seeks to ensure that no more species of wild birds are lost from the UK.

It also monitors and responds to development proposals and carries out research on wild-bird populations. It ensures the laws protecting wild birds are enforced and believes education to be vitally important, especially for young people.

To help the RSPB with its work, write to RSPB, The Lodge, Sandy, Bedfordshire SG19 2DL.

THE BRITISH TRUST FOR ORNITHOLOGY

The BTO aims to promote and encourage the wider understanding, appreciation and conservation of wild birds through scientific studies.

The trust co-ordinates most of the national schemes for monitoring wild-bird populations, including the National Ringing Scheme, the Nest Record Scheme, the Breeding Bird Survey and the Common Bird Census. Through these schemes the BTO involves thousands of amateur bird-watchers whose records contribute to an invaluable picture of bird populations and on which much of today's conservation activities are based.

To support the BTO, or to take part in some of their surveys, write to BTO, The Nunnery, Thetford, Norfolk IP24 2PU.

THE WILDLIFE TRUSTS

The Wildlife Trusts are a nationwide network of local trusts which work to protect wildlife in town and country. Through its care of 2,000 local nature reserves the trusts are dedicated to the achievement of a country richer in wildlife managed on sustainable principles.

To find out about your local trust ask at your local library or write to The Wildlife Trusts, The Green, Witham Park, Waterside South, Lincoln LN5 7JR.

Index